WHAT THE KNOWERS OF ALLĀH HAVE SAID ABOUT THE KNOWLEDGE OF ALLĀH

First published in 2014 by

Fayda Books
3695F Cascade Rd
Atlanta, GA 30331

http://www.faydabooks.com
Email: orders@faydabooks.com

ISBN 9780991381333

Cover design
MUHAMMADAN PRESS
mail@muhammadanpress.com

Typesetting
ETHEREA DESIGN
enquiries@ethereadesign.com

Printed and bound in the United States

Thanks to Khalid and Ainun Ajmain, and Light of Eminence publications for the original proofreading and publication of the English text as part of the book, Knowing Allah, Living Islam.

What the Knowers of Allāh Have Said About the Knowledge of Allāh

Imam Cheikh Tidiane Ali Cissé

Celebration of the Prophet's Birthday,
Abidjan, Ivory Coast, 2011

Translated by

ZAKARIYA WRIGHT &
MUHAMMAD HASSIEM ABDULLAHI

FAYDA BOOKS

Contents

Introduction to the Translation 7

What the Knowers of Allāh Have Said About the Knowledge of Allāh 13

The Reality of the Knowledge of Allāh 15

The Path to Gnosis 23

The Doctrine of Unity among the Gnostics 29

The Need for Companionship with a Gnostic 35

The Comportment (adab) of the Perfected Actualized Gnostic Sages 43

Bewilderment and Surrender 47

The Veil (al-ḥijāb) 51

Entering the Holy Presence 57

Qur'an Verses and Prophetic statements explaining Gnosis 59

The Claim of the Cessation of Spiritual Training in the earlier generations and the Response of the Ṣāḥib al-Fayḍa 63

The Tijānī Sufi path and the Way of Gnosis 75

Breaths of Lights in the statements of Allāh's Exalted Folk 85

Introduction to the Translation

Cheikh Tidiane Cissé (or Shaykh Tijānī b. ʿAlī Sīsī) holds the Imamate of the Grand Mosque in Medina-Baye Kaolack, Senegal. As Imam of the spiritual heart for the followers of Shaykh Ibrāhīm Niasse, Cheikh Tidiane Cissé is the teacher and guide of millions of Muslims around the world. He succeeds to the position after a lifetime of personal instruction and companionship with some of the twentieth century's most eminent Tijānī scholars: Shaykh Ibrāhīm Niasse (d. 1975), Shaykh Sayyid ʿAlī Cissé (d. 1982), and Shaykh Ḥasan b. ʿAlī Cissé (d. 2008). Upon succeeding to the Imamate in 2008, Cheikh Tidiane also assumed leadership of the humanitarian NGO founded by Shaykh Ḥasan Cissé, the African American Islamic Institute. Cheikh Tidiane Cissé has attained wide renown as an Islamic scholar, a Sufi guide, and a committed humanitarian activist.

Cheikh Tidiane Cissé (b. 1955) is the second son of Shaykh Ibrāhīm's most beloved student, Shaykh 'Alī Cissé, and his first daughter, Fāṭima Zahra Niasse. After memorizing Qur'ān in Medina-Baye, Shaykh Tijani himself became a Qur'ān teacher in Medina Baye while continuing his Islamic studies. In his late teens, he devoted himself full-time to personalized instruction (*majālis al-ʿilm*), first under his father, Shaykh ʿAlī (1971-1972); and then under his grandfather, Shaykh Ibrāhīm (1973). He was the last to be personally instructed by Shaykh Ibrāhīm in the classical texts, focusing mostly on Arabic literature and poetry. He would later receive the highest of licenses from his father, Shaykh ʿAlī Cissé, who told him: "Whatever Shaykh Ibrāhīm gave me, I am giving you."

Cheikh Tidiane's collection of scholarly licenses (*majmūʿ ījāzāt*) thus includes comprehensive authorizations in the Islamic sciences of Qur'ān recitation (*tajwīd*) and exegesis (*tafsīr*), Prophetic traditions (*ḥadīth*), jurisprudence (*fiqh*) and its principles (*uṣūl*), theology (*ʿaqīda*), and literature (*adab*). The chains of transmission in this collection pass through Shaykh Ibrāhīm to some of the most prominent Islamic scholars around the world in the twentieth century. These scholars, by whom Shaykh Ibrāhīm was invested personally, include: ʿAbd al-Ḥayy al-Kattānī (Morocco), Muḥammad al-Ḥafiẓ al-Tijānī (Egypt), Aḥmad Sukayrij (Morocco), Ṣāliḥ b. al-Fuḍayl (Tunisia, Saudi Arabia), ʿAbd-Allāh b. al-Ṭayyib al-Azharī (Egypt), Muḥammad al-Amīn al-ʿAlawī (Mauritania), and his own father, ʿAbd-Allāh b. Muḥammad Niasse (Senegal). The authorizations in Sufism (*taṣawwuf*) transmitted to Cheikh Tidiane through Shaykh Ibrāhīm are similarly comprehensive. It has been related that the renowned Indonesian Ḥadīth scholar of Mecca, Yāsīn al-Fādānī (d. 1990), granted comprehensive authorization (*ijāzā*) to Cheikh Tidiane, along with Shaykh Ḥasan Cissé, in Mecca by order of the Prophet Muḥammad in a visionary encounter.

Upon completion of his early education in Senegal, he traveled to Egypt where he lived with Shaykh Ḥasan Cissé during his elder brother's last year of study in Cairo. Like his brother, Shaykh Tijani excelled in his formal studies in Egypt; the result, he said, of the rigor of the informal instruction given him in Senegal. He graduated first in his class in the

Azhar preparatory school, receiving his diploma in Arabic language in 1974. He received his Baccalaureate in 1977 in Arabic Language, graduating fourth in his class. By 1981, he had distinguished himself at the University of Azhar with a degree in the faculty of Uṣūl al-Dīn (Theology), specializing in Ḥadīth (Prophetic Traditions).

After finishing his studies in Egypt, he traveled extensively throughout Africa, the Middle East and America, attending conferences, participating in religious debates, and calling people to Islam. He edited and published several important works, including Shaykh Ibrāhīm's *Kāshif al-ilbās* and an edited collection of Shaykh Ibrāhīm's writings, which he named *Saʿādat al-anām*. He also aided the publication of a comprehensive collection of Shaykh Ibrāhīm's supplications, *Kanz al-Maṣūn*. Most recently, he has edited and published the most important work of the Tijāniyya, the *Jawāhir al-maʿānī*, based on the original manuscript of ʿAlī Harāzim al-Barāda currently in Cheikh Tidiane's possession.

Such invaluable work has not gone unnoticed. One Azhar scholar reportedly told him that his work identifying ḥadīth citations in the 2001 publication of *Kāshif al-ilbās* would have been enough to earn him a doctoral degree at Azhar University. In the introduction to Cheikh Tidiane's reprinting of the *Kāshif*, Shaykh Ḥasan Cissé wrote: "I thank my dear brother, the master, the Shaykh, Tijānī 'Alī Cissé, who spent of his efforts for the success of this pious work and much appreciated endeavor."

The high scholarship and humanitarian mission of Cheikh Tidiane Cissé have garnered recognition around the world. The Senegalese government appointed him as Senegal's General Commissioner for the Hajj in 2001. In 2006, he was again recognized by Senegalese President Aboulaye Wade and appointed a Senegalese "Special Missions Ambassador." He has also received Senegal's distinguished award, the

Ordre de Merite (1993). On a recent trip to Atlanta, Georgia (January, 2011), he received the city's prestigious Phoenix Award. A 2014/2015 report issued by Jordan's Royal Islamic Strategic Studies Centre and Georgetown University's Center for Muslim-Christian Understanding ranks Cheikh Tidiane thirteenth among the world's 500 most influential Muslim personalities.

The work presented here was originally written for delivery at a Mawlid celebration in Abidjan, Ivory Coast in 2011. It concerns *maʿrifat-Allāh*, the experiential knowledge of God, sometimes translated as gnosis or cognizance. *Maʿrifa* is often considered the essence of the Sufi path, for it meant to actualize the last stage of the Islamic religion: after *al-islām* (submission) and *al-īmān* (faith) comes al-iḥsān (excellence), "to worship God as if you are seeing Him, and if you are not seeing Him, know that He is seeing you."

ZAKARIYA WRIGHT

What the Knowers of Allāh Have Said About the Knowledge of Allāh

Imam Cheikh Tidiane Ali Cissé

Celebration of the Prophet's Birthday,
Abidjan, Ivory Coast, 2011

Translated by

ZAKARIYA WRIGHT &
MUHAMMAD HASSIEM ABDULLAHI

FAYDA BOOKS

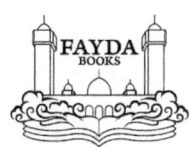

بِسْمِ ٱللَّهِ ٱلرَّحْمَٰنِ ٱلرَّحِيمِ

In the Name of Allāh the Compassionate the Merciful

All praise belongs to Allāh, who engendered fraternity between the souls before the appearance of bodies. We have learned from the words of Allāh's Prophet that the souls (*arwāḥ*) are like soldiers standing in rank. Those who knew each other before feel affinity in this realm and those who do not have differences. Allāh the Most High said, "And when your Lord took the children of Adam, from their loins, their descendants, and made them testify [saying to them], 'Am I not your Lord?' And they said, 'Yes indeed (*balā*)!'"[1] So they responded with the letter *bā*ʾ, out of which was what was, out of which is what is until the Day of Gathering.

May the prayer and peace of Allāh be upon the secret of the Divine Essence (*dhāt*), the light of the Divine Essence, our master Muḥammad, the light of existence (*wujūd*), the spiritual support (*madad*) of existence. There is no existence except his existence, no light except his light, no spiritual support except his support. And by this prayer, we come to the knowledge of him. The Lord of Might said, "I was an unknown treasure. Then I desired to be known, so I created the creation and made myself known to them. So by Me (*fa-bī*) they know Me." And the letters of the word, "by Me" (*fa-bī*) are equivalent to ninety-two, and these are

1 Qur'an, 7:172.

also the numerological equivalent of the letters in the name "Muḥammad."[2] That is to say: it was by Muḥammad that the Exalted and Blessed Lord made Himself known. And may this prayer be on his pure family, his chosen companions, and those who have succeeded them in spiritual excellence (*iḥsān*) till the Day of Judgment.

Distinguished leaders, ministers, princes, and directors; happy companions; distinguished imams, shaykhs, and instructors; his excellency, the noble, eminent master, the scholarly Sharīf ʿUmar b. ʿAbd al-ʿAzīz, who has taken responsibility for this blessed gathering, together with his noble brothers; to all you brothers and sisters gathered here from all corners of the earth in order to celebrate the birthday of the Prophet: may Allāh's peace, mercy, and blessing be upon you all.

Allāh has facilitated my coming to this blessed place to meet with this large gathering of beloveds, among the citizens of the Ivory Coast and neighboring countries. Our purpose is to discuss what is between us concerning "the knowledge of Allāh" (*maʿrifa bi-Llāh*). The Sufi path, it is said, consists of both (individual) remembrance (*dhikr*) and collective reminding (*madhākara*). We hope that Allāh the Most High benefits us by what we hear, and allows us to hear what benefits us, in our final destination back to Him. He responds to those who long for Him. So by Him do I speak, and my words are only by Him, from Him and to Him.

---

2 In Arabic, *fāʾ*=80, *bāʾ*=2, *yāʾ*=10; *mīm*=40, *ḥāʾ*=8, *dāl*=4. Thus 80+2+10=92; and 40+8+40+4=92. For a reference chart concerning this system of numerology, see Annemarie Schimmel, *Mystical Dimensions of Islam* (Chapel Hill, UNC Press, 1975), xix-xx.

The Reality of the Knowledge of Allāh

Imam Abū al-Qāsim ʿAbd al-Karīm b. Hūzān al-Qushayrī,[3] may Allāh be pleased with him, described the knowledge of Allāh as follows:

> Cognizance (*maʿrifa*) is knowledge (ʿilm), for every knowing (ʿilm) is an awareness (*maʿrifa*), and every awareness is a knowing. Every knowledgeable person of God (*ʿālim bi-Llāh*) is thus a gnostic, and every gnostic (*ʿārif*) is a scholar (*ʿālim*). In the terminology of the Sufis, gnosis is attributed to the one who knows the Real, Glorious is He, by His Names and His Attributes, whom God has then confirmed in his affairs. Then God purifies him from his lowly traits and awakens him. Long he waits at the door in God's attendance, his heart persisting in worldly withdrawal, until Allāh the Most High grants him the beauty of acceptance in His presence. Allāh then confirms him in all of his words, and cuts off from him the stray thoughts of his self (*nafs*). Nothing occurs to his heart that would invite him to other than Allāh. So he becomes a stranger to the creation, absolved from the negligence of his self, and purified from fixations and petty observations. He persists in the secret of his

3 ʿAbd al-Karīm Abū l-Qāsim al-Qushayrī (d. 1072) was an early Sufi master from Khurasan.

> intimate discourse with Allāh the Exalted. He ascertains the reality of every moment as having its return to Allāh. The Real, Glorious is He, informs him (of each moment) beforehand, and permeates him with an awareness of through an awareness the secrets of Allāh's dispositions and capacities. It is at this point that he is named "gnostic" (*ᶜārif*), and his spiritual state is called "gnosis" (*maᶜrifa*). The gist of the matter is that a person obtains gnosis by his Lord to the extent of his alienation from his self.[4]

The Prophet David (Dāwūd), upon him be peace, once asked, "O Lord! How do I arrive to You?" The Lord, exalted is His majesty, said, "Leave your self, and come."

The hidden pole, our master Aḥmad al-Tijānī, may Allāh be pleased with him, was asked about the reality of knowing Allāh the Most High. He responded saying:

> True gnosis is when Allāh takes a servant in such an embrace that he does not know origin (*aṣl*), differentiation (*faṣl*), or means (*sabab*). He does not discern a specified wherewithal, and nothing remains of his sensory feeling, individual witnessing, personal erasure, movement, or volition. What has befallen him by divine manifestation (*tajalla*) has no beginning and no end; it is not bound by delimitation or ending.

In the *Jawāhir al-maᶜānī*, he also said, "The people of gnosis are absent in Allāh from everything that perishes. They see by the majesty and beauty of Allāh, and they know by His attributes and names.

The pole of gnostics, the bringer of the Tijānī flood (*ṣāḥib al-fayḍa al-Tijāniyya*), our master Shaykh Ibrāhīm Niasse, said:

---

4 Abū l-Qāsim al-Qushayrī, *Risālat al-Qushayrīya*; For an English translation of this epistle in full, see Qushayri's "Treatise on Sufism" in John Renard, *Knowledge of God in Classical Sufism* (New York: Paulist Press, 2004), 286-293. The translation above is our own.

> Gnosis is the rooting and establishment of the spirit (*rūḥ*) in the presence of witnessing, with complete annihilation and persistence by Allāh. The gnostic for the Sufi people is the one who sees in otherness the essence, or who witnesses the Real in otherness. For me, the gnostic is he who becomes annihilated in Allāh's Essential Being (*dhāt*) once, then becomes annihilated in Allāh's Attribute (*ṣifa*) twice or three times, and then becomes annihilated in the Name once. So he attests to the creation by the three realities (*ḥaqā'iq*), and he attests to the names by the Name. This is a spiritual station without which there is only the gummy sap of thorny shrubs and the crumbling of hearts. It cannot be obtained by the giving of money or (having lots of) children. Who has mastered this station is possessed of perfect wakefulness. He is perfectly content with Allāh, with His wisdom, with His rulings, and with the entirety of His decrees. And Allāh is pleased with him, and he becomes deserving of His words, "*So enter among my righteous servants, and enter My Paradise*" (Qur'ān, 89:29-30).

He also said, may Allāh be pleased with him, that gnosis means, "the unveiling (*kashf*) of Allāh's names and attributes, and the result of this is the observance of Allāh and the sincerity of action for His sake." And he said, "The reality of gnosis is the witnessing of the perfection of Allāh's Essential Being (*dhāt*): '*And there is nothing the like comparable to Him*' (42:11)." And he also said, "The one acquainted with Allāh does not derive pleasure from anything else in the creation, and the one acquainted with the lower world (*dunyā*) has no pleasure in his life. Who has opened for the him the eye of sight is astonished into silence, and does not occupy himself with words."

The Greatest Shaykh Muḥyī al-Dīn Ibn ʿArabī said: "Know that gnosis is of two types: general gnosis, and special gnosis. As for the first, this is the gnosis obtained by seeking evidence, and it is called 'certain knowledge' (*ʿilm al-yaqīn*).

As for the second, it has two types: the 'eye of certainty' (*ʿayn al-yaqīn*) and knowledge of the 'absolute truth' (*ḥaqq al-yaqīn*). This first is gnosis obtained by means of witnessing, and it is the station of the elite saints. The second is gnosis the spirit obtains by the One witnessed. This is when the senses of the heart become tranquil of the self's turbidities, freed from the chains of carnality, and purified from base human characteristics. At this point the knowledge of Allāh the Exalted becomes manifest to the spirit."

(Abū Bakr) al-Shiblī said, "The gnostic does not look to other than Him. He does not speak words by other than Him. He does not see any guardian for himself other than Allāh the Exalted."

Some of the Sufi people have said, "Gnosis is when the Real causes you to die to your self, and brings you to life by Him." And it is said, "The gnostic becomes intimate with the remembrance of Allāh, and flees from the creation. He presents his needs to Allāh, and Allāh makes him independent of His creation. He humbles himself before the Most High, and then Allāh exalts him among His creation."

Abū al-Ṭayyib al-Sāmirī said: "Gnosis is the Real's sunrise upon the secret, innermost being through the arrival of lights." And it has been said, "The gnostic is more that what is said, the scholar is less than what is said."

Junayd said, "The gnostic is he to whom Allāh has enunciated His secret, and he has kept quiet."[5]

Yaʿqūb al-Sūsī was asked, "Does the gnostic feel grief on account of anything other than Allāh the Mighty and Majestic?" He said, "Does he see anything besides Him on whose account to be grieved?" Then he was asked, "By what eye does he look at things?" He said, "With the eye of annihilation and perishing."

---

5 An alternative translation of this statement could be, "The Real speaks from the innermost being (*sirr*) of the gnostic, while he remains silent."

It has been said, "The gnostic is the one whose eye cries, but whose heart laughs."

Junayd said, "The gnostic is not knowledgeable until he is like the earth, enclosing both righteousness and corruption, or like the cloud shading everything, or like the rain quenching the thirst of those it loves and those it does not love."

Abū Yazīd (al-Bisṭāmī) said, "They have obtained gnosis by forsaking what belongs to them, and stopping with what belongs to Him."

Ibn ʿAṭāʾ-Allāh said, "Gnosis is based on three pillars: fear (*hayba*), modesty (*hayya*), and intimacy with Allāh (*uns*)."

It was said to Dhū l-Nūn al-Miṣrī, "How did you come to know your Lord?" He said, "I came to know my Lord by my Lord, and if not for my Lord, I would not have known my Lord."

It has been said, "The scholar is a good example, but the gnostic is the one to be followed."

One of the shaykhs was asked, "How did you come to know Allāh the Exalted?" He said, "By a light shining forth from the tongue, taken from the differentiated one contracted (with Allāh's secret), and the expression passing from the tongue of one destroyed, lost; pointing towards the finding of a (divine) manifestation, preferring the secret over everything else. This is how it came to be." And there are many other expressions of this sort. As the poet has said:

I uttered without utterance; He is the utterance
For You is the pronouncing of the utterance, or to explain out of the utterance
You appeared where before You had been hidden
A flash of lightning burst upon me, and I burst forth with speech.

It has been said of the gnostic's description: "Nothing makes him impure, and everything is purified by him."

Dhū l-Nūn al-Miṣrī said, "The signs of the gnostic are three: the light of his gnosis does not obscure the light of his pious restraint (*waraᶜ*); he does not believe that inner, esoteric knowledge (*ᶜilm al-bāṭin*) abolishes the need to follow outward legal injunctions; and the many gifts and blessings given to him by Allāh does not incite him to expose the veils that cover Allāh›s hidden sanctity."

Abū Saᶜīd al-Kharrāz (al-Baghdādī) said, "Gnosis comes from an eye that weeps abundantly, and from expending the utmost effort."

Junayd was asked about the saying of Dhū l-Nūn al-Miṣrī describing the gnostic, "He was here but now he has gone." Junayd replied, "One spiritual state does not hold the gnostic back from another spiritual state, and one spiritual station does not veil him from changing stations. Thus he is with the people of every place just as they are, he experiences whatever they experience, and he speaks their language so that they might benefit by his speech."

Muḥammad b. al-Faḍl said, "Gnosis is the life of the heart with Allāh."

Ibn al-Sammāk was asked, "When does the servant know that he has attained the reality of gnosis?" He answered, "When the servant comes to witness the Real with the eye of esteem and respect, and when he passes away from everything other than Him."

Yaḥya b. Muᶜādh, may Allāh have mercy on him, said, "Gnosis is the proximity of the heart to the Ever Near (*al-Qarīb*), the spirit's vigilant awareness of the Beloved (*al-Ḥabīb*), and the isolation of oneself from everything else with the Sovereign responsive to prayers (*al-Mālik al-mujīb*)."

It has been narrated that Allāh the Exalted once revealed to the Prophet Dāwūd, peace be upon him, "O

Dāwūd! Come to know Me and come to know yourself!" So Dāwūd meditated on these words and said, "My God! I have come to know You through Your transcendental uniqueness (*fardaniyya*), might (*qudra*) and everlasting permanence (*baqā*ʾ); and I have come to know myself through my incapacity (*ʿajz*) and annihilation (*fanā*ʾ)."

The knowledge of Allāh, glorious and exalted is He, is, according to these meanings, the utmost goal and aspiration of the ascetics and the highest degree that the God-conscious hope to attain. Thus, the Sufi people have been thrust on to the path of obtaining this most precious and invaluable acquisition. They have spent their lives in its pursuit, leaving their homelands on its account, undergoing extreme difficulties and passing through severe ordeals until they achieved victory in its attainment. Some of them have turned back empty handed from failing to fulfill its prerequisites or patiently endure its weighty affair, without realizing anything of its reality. It is enough for you as an example to recall the story of Prophet Moses (Mūsa) and his companion, Khiḍr, peace be upon them both. Mūsa was among the arch-Prophets. But he could not bear patiently with the testing and examination of Khiḍr. So he had to return without obtaining anything of this Divine Knowledge (*ʿilm al-ladunī*), although he went on the journey with the express intention of acquiring such knowledge.

This is why this knowledge has been referred to as "the rarest treasure" and the one in possession of it has been referred to as "the philosophers stone" or "the red sulphur" (*al-kibrīt al-aḥmar*). However, since the appearance of the Saintly Seal (Shaykh Aḥmad al-Tijānī), the distance to its arrival has been folded up and made short. The knowledge has been spread among the people of his spiritual path and circulated among his followers. And with the appearance of the bringer of the Tijani flood—our master Shaykh Ibrāhīm

b. al-Ḥājj ʿAbd-Allāh Niasse—there has been an effusion of Divine knowledge and gnosis. Everyone has drunk from its contents, until the knowledge of Allāh has spread to nearly every land. All who have a connection with this honorable saintly pole (*quṭb*) has been blessed with their share, and none have been given a greater portion than them in this day-and-age. Such people are scholars, leaders, imams and princes. They are stars and lamps of guidance in every land.

The Path to Gnosis

The bringer of the Tijani spiritual flood, our master Shaykh Ibrāhīm Niasse quoted (in his book *Kāshif al-ilbās*) the distinguished scholar and knower of Allāh, Sidi Muḥammad al-Yadālī from his *Sharḥ khātimat al-ṭaṣawwuf*:

> It has been said that the quickest way to enter the Divine Presence is through the remembrance of Allāh (*dhikr*), because the Name is inseparable from the One named. Since the one engaged in remembrance ceaselessly mentions the Name of Allāh, the veils are torn to shreds bit by bit, until the heart comes to witness Allāh directly. When this happens, the spiritual aspirant dispenses with the remembrance due to his witnessing the One remembered. So this is what the Sufi people mean by entering the Divine Presence of Allāh: the removal of veils so that you enter the Divine Presence while you remain sitting in your place.

Al-Yadālī also said in *Sharh shahiyyat al-samā*ᶜ:

> A servant does not draw near to His Exalted Presence unless he displays a deep ense of modest shame and bashfulness. He does not perfect this (disposition) unless he obtains spiritual illumination (*kashf*) and the lifting of the veils; and he does not perfect this unless he

perseveres in the remembrance. Constant engagement in the remembrance is the only way to perfect the station of complete sincerity, where one sees all actions as the creation of Allāh. There is no other way to cut off the evil, satanic thoughts, nor are the egocentric delusions weakened by any other means. The continued practice of the remembrance causes the anxiety and sadness with the world to disappear, for such emotions are only a result of the heedlessness of Allāh. Indeed, the servant has no one to blame but himself if anxieties and sorrows should afflict him in unrelenting succession, for these are only the consequence of turning away from his Lord. He who desires persistent happiness must devote himself to persistent remembrance.

Some of the deluded and misguided folk have become stagnant, contenting themselves with the gatherings of remembrance (*majlis al-dhikr*) in the morning and evening, while remaining heedless of Allāh in between. But this practice is of no use for the spiritual wayfarer (*sālik*) who seeks the station of the Sufi people. Perhaps he who contends with this will cite the Prophetic saying: "If the servant remembers his Lord for a time at the beginning and end of the day, he will be forgiven whatever comes between." However, forgiveness does not include spiritual advancement (*tarqiya*). The result of forgiveness is (simply) to equate him with the one who has obeyed Allah. Understand that the desire of the Sufi people is continuous spiritual elevation with each breath, through the remembrance of Allāh, so that they do not regard themselves as having fulfilled one atom of Allāh's right on them.

Gnosis with the Sufi people is the acquisition of the knowledge of God as it relates to His Essential Being, Attributes, Names and Actions. This is the most important of the religious obligations and the most sublime honor, as it is the foundation of the faith and the goal of Islam. The gnosis of Allāh is the utmost goal in the perfection of the human condition, the highest rank of spiritual realization, and the most cherished ideal. None obtains the rank of Divine gnosis except that he has been allowed through all of the journey's waystations with firm step, strong faith, and sound heart. The knowledgeable one of Allāh does not have knowledge until he folds up the waystations of the path to Allāh. Mankind's knowledge of Allāh is above all other types of knowledge.

None is given the strength to attain this degree unless he has begun his journey with correct comportment (*adab*), for the rectitude of his external and internal states depends on the proper conduct. He then obtains what is desired in both his deeds and words, without discomfort or effort. His attributes are perfected, a completion of the light of Divine Perfection. Such a person is elevated from perfection to a greater perfection. From proper comportment, his character acquires light. He is illumined with guidance, and the Real causes him to shed light. His spirit is nurtured with the rubies of realities. He consecrates himself to Allāh, with utter sincerity in the religion for His sake. His heart blooms with faith, and his intention is purified externally and internally.

Who knows Allāh, with the gnosis that befits Him, walks among the creation as the symbol for the excellences of the most exalted attributes. He is of the best comportment in his words, actions, and spiritual state. He desires good for his brother in faith, the same as he desires for himself. He directs himself to Allāh with a pure heart, mature belief, firm faith, feet firmly planted, and with elevated spiritual experience. His goal is Allāh. The Shaykh of Islam, our master Shaykh Ibrāhīm Niasse said:

> The quickest way to achieve gnosis is by following the Messenger of Allāh, may the peace and blessings of Allāh be upon him, in his statements, actions, spiritual states, and character, and in discharging the rights of Allāh publicly and privately. He has absolute sincerity with

> Allāh the Exalted, without any worldly or otherworldly motive. He is like this only for the sake of Allāh the Exalted, glorifying and exalting Him. He does this with open pleasure, submission, trust, and dependence on Allāh the Exalted for every single thing.

The consummate scholar, Sīdī Muḥammad b. al-Mishrī al-Sabāʿī al-Sāʾihī, related a narration concerning the Hidden Pole Sīdī Aḥmad al-Tijānī in the book, *Rawḍ al-muḥibb al-fānī*:

> As for the true reality of the Shaykh of Arrival (*shaykh al-wāṣil*), he is the one for whom all of the veils have been removed from the perfect beholding of the Divine Presence, with visual perception and certain realization. The process begins with attentive awareness (*muḥāḍara*), which entails observing the realities from behind a thick curtain. Next comes disclosure (*mukāshifa*), which entails observing the realities from behind a thin curtain. Then comes direct witnessing (*mushāhada*), which entails the manifestation of the realities without a veil (*hijāb*), but with particularity. Last comes the direct beatific vision, which entails observing the realities without veil or particularity, with absolutely no surviving trace of otherness. This is the station of eradication, destruction, annihilation, and the annihilation of annihilation.
>
> There is nothing in this station except the direct vision of the Real, in the Real, for the Real, and by the Real.
>
> *So nothing remains except Allāh, and nothing besides Him.*
> *There is nothing to be added and nothing to be separated.*
>
> Then comes real life and true existence, in which one is able to distinguish the degrees on the basis of direct experiential knowledge (*maʿrifa*) of their particularities,

requirements, exigencies and everything to which they are entitled. One will know, as well, the source for each degree, the reason for its existence, its intended purpose, and the return of its affairs. This is the station of the servant's comprehension of his personal identity and his knowledge of all its secrets and particularities; as well as his knowledge of the Divine Presence, Its grandeur, majesty, exalted attributes and perfection. And this knowledge of his will be the product of direct experience and indubitable vision.

Vast deserts must be traversed for the holder of such a degree. In spite of hardships, the effort is perfectly worthwhile, since the Real has granted him a specific authorization (*idhn*) to provide right guidance to His servants and has charged him with the task of directing them towards the Divine Presence.

The Doctrine of Unity among the Gnostics

The consummate scholar Sīdī Muḥammad b. al-Mishrī reported in *Rawḍ al-muḥibb al-fānī*:

> Shaykh Aḥmad al-Tijānī was asked about the doctrine of unity among the gnostics (*tawḥīd al-ʿārifīn*), and its difference with the doctrine of unity among the speculative theologians (*tawḥīd al-mutakallimīn*). He responded, may Allāh be pleased with him, by saying:
> "As for the *tawḥīd* of the speculative theologians, they have offered a sort of warning for (maintaining) the health of *tawḥīd*, demonstrating what constitutes incapacity, imperfection or ignorance in the description of the Creator, glorious and exalted is He. They have offered all of this with rational proofs based on what has been firmly established. But these theologians find themselves in great difficulty from the plethora of successive analogies. One should not occupy oneself with this type of *tawḥīd*, due to the abundance of doubt and delirium therein.
>
> "As for the *tawḥīd* of the gnostics, this is the worship of One God, with contentment and submission to the judgment of One God. In all of their conditions, they depend only on the One God. They direct their aspirations and their hearts only to the One God. They

have no longing except for One God alone. Their goal in the beginning, middle and end of his journey is only for the One God.

"All of this is through the dismissal of passion (*hawa*) externally and internally, in both its essence and its traces. The servant is at the remotest distance from the wrappings of the ego (*nafs*), passion, and Satan. If there should occur to him the slightest inclination towards passion, even the smallest grain or speck of dust, he is not among those who ascribe oneness to the One God, and he cannot be described as having worshipped One God. So if they have this sort of *tawḥīd*, they build for it a fortress and become established in it. They become drowned in the ocean of Divine satisfaction and submission, knowing from Him that nothing escapes the rule (*ḥukm*) of the One God, the sweetness and the bitterness, the good and the bad. No one has any choice along with Him, for if there were a choice other than His, there would be a god beside Him.

"Who has correctly implemented the aforementioned descriptions is at ease with whatever affliction. He sits on the carpet of tranquility and comfort, with a robe of honor that melts away the difficulty, the misfortune of self-direction, in which he was previously engaged. There he sits with Allāh on the carpet of proximity and intimacy. He does not need to beg for what he finds of provision, gifts, wealth, the fulfillment of all desires. All this is from Allāh's might, majesty, and bestowal of honor, for which there is no limit or enumeration.

"So this is the *tawḥīd* of the gnostics referred to by the saintly pole Mawlay ʿAbd al-ʿAzīz al-Dabbāgh, may Allāh be pleased with him. He said it was being free from the difficulty of defending analogies successively piled up by the theologians. The *tawḥīd* of the gnostics does not cling to analogies."

Then Shaykh al-Tijani, may Allāh be pleased with him, said, "The likeness of this is as two people. One of them is deeply afflicted by sickness. As soon as one sickness leaves him, one greater comes to take its place.

So he devotes his attention to searching for cures, to knowing each sickness, its sources, causes, and remedy. But how can he obtain this, given his defective state, limited time, isolation, and constitution? For he finds himself in great difficulty comprehending these sciences, and every time he makes a mistake in anything, harm afflicts him. He wastes most of his aspiration occupied with these sciences.

"As for the other person, he comes forth in perfect health and strength. Allāh secures him from pestilence and affliction. No sickness befalls him. Since he does not himself see any sickness, he is unaware of the knowledge of medicine, and of all of its exigencies and aggravating circumstances.

"So the first one says to the other one, 'Your ignorance of medicine is the source of great harm!' But the other one says to the first, 'Only those like you, infected with sickness, require medicine. As for me, I am not sick, so I have no need of medicine.'"

Then he was asked, "Why has this *tawḥīd* not appeared in books and poetry collections to provide benefit to everyone?"

He said, "The answer is that the gnostics have not hidden it, for this *tawḥīd* was that sent with all of the Messengers, and it was this which was manifested to the generality of the creation. But the theologians left this and studied a way to deny this *tawḥīd* from the general population. This was for the purpose of inclining them to the useless saddlebags of theology, its rules and methodology, by means of rational proofs and demonstrations. Among them there were those who thought that this was the height of proximity to Allāh the Exalted and the perfection of knowledge. But they did not know that this was misguidance, and that it had placed them in the farthest distance from Allāh.

"The reason that the common folk fell into the confusion of the theologians was their coming upon the earlier sciences of philosophy. Philosophy became established in their knowledge as the 'science of *tawḥīd*.'

The truth is that the search for Divine knowledge through rational laws and logical demonstrations is the means by which Allāh removed them from the knowledge of the Real, from approaching with that which draws near to Allāh, and from the awareness of His Majesty.

"When this third knowledge of philosophy entered the hearts, and they heard this as the discipline of *tawḥīd*, these saddlebags, articulated now in Arabic, changed them from the people of Divine favor to those who rejected Allāh the Exalted. Generally, all who obtained this science leaped into ignorance, while claiming that they had reached the pinnacle of knowledge. But they were far removed from the knowledge of Allāh and the awareness of His Majesty.

"They expounded to the common folk that whoever did not know their science was as if he knew nothing. The souls of the common folk followed them, inclined towards bounty, for they saw how they were exalted in the hearts of the commoners, kings, and princes. On account of following this whirlwind, which differed from the righteous forefathers (*salaf*) without any excuse or restraint, the true knowledge of *tawḥīd* sent with the Messengers was forgotten. Those who sought the *tawḥīd* of the Messengers came to reject the *tawḥīd* of the philosophers as poison for the Sufis and gnostics. And indeed, those who sought the *tawḥīd* of the philosophers became as poison for theology itself.

"As for the interjection into the discipline of theology by gnostics such as al-Ashʿarī and al-Sanūsī and their like, may Allāh be pleased with them, it was only their desire for kindness with the common folk. When it was (argued) that (disputes over) the *tawḥīd* of the Messengers cannot be answered except by the sword, they answered that the common people could accept the command of Allāh by their own volition if they were given foundational rational proofs (for the correct *tawḥīd*). They saw that this was better than the sword, for the one forced by the sword does not enter the religion except under compulsion and force. So this was the

> reason for their interjection into the science of theology." As for the "Unity of Existence" (*waḥdat al-wujūd*), his words on that subject will be presented later on.

Imam al-Ghazālī, may Allāh have mercy on him, divided *tawḥīd* into four degrees in his *Iḥyā ʿulūm al-dīn*: the core, the core of the core, the shell, and the shell of the shell. He said:

> The first degree of *tawḥīd* is when a person says with his tongue, "There is no god but Allāh." But his heart is heedless of the statement, or even in denial of it, as with the *tawḥīd* of the hypocrites. The second degree is when the heart testifies to the meaning of the articulation, as with the testimony of the generality of Muslims. This is the belief of the common people. The third is when a person witnesses *tawḥīd* by way of spiritual unveiling (*kashf*) through the light of the Real. This is the station of those drawn near. They see many things, but despite the multiplicity, they see all as having originated from the One, the Compeller. The fourth degree is when a person does not see anything in existence except the One. This is the witnessing of the most truthful ones (*ṣiddīqūn*). The Sufis call this the annihilation (*fanāʾ*) in *tawḥīd*. This is because when such a person sees nothing but the One, he does not see himself. As he does not see himself due to his complete absorption in *tawḥīd*, (it is correct to say) he has passed away from himself in *tawḥīd*. The meaning here is that he has become annihilated to the vision of himself, and of creation entirely.

Muḥammad b. Mūsa al-Wāsiṭī said, "All forms of *tawḥīd* that are articulated by tongues, explained in (inevitable) aggrandizement, abstraction, or separation (*tafrīd*), are infected with sickness. The reality is other than that."

Our master and our Shaykh Aḥmad al-Tijānī, may Allāh be pleased with him, said: "As long as you see that you exist and that Allāh exists, so that there are two, where is the Oneness (*tawḥīd*)? Oneness only exists if the Oneness is by Allāh, from Allāh, and to Allāh. The servant does not enter into it nor exit from it. And this is not realized except by way of annihilation (*fanā*ʾ)."

If it were established that the Real were separate from the existence (*wujūd*), He would be "missing" (*mafqūd*), and beyond your aspiration. Ibn ʿAjība explained the words in the *Ḥikam* (of Ibn ʿAṭāʾ-Allāh), "Let not the intention of your aspiration be shifted to other than Him, for ones hopes cannot exceed the Generous Lord (*al-Karīm*)." He said, "O aspirant! Bind your aspirations and desires to Allāh, nothing besides Him. He is always Generous, and His blessing flows night and day. The Generous Lord is not exceeded by hopes, and He loves to be asked so that He may answer."

The Need for Companionship with a Gnostic

Know that the aspirant does not benefit from the knowledge and spiritual states of the shaykh unless he submits to him with complete obedience, believing in his excellence and completion. He must stop where the shaykh orders him to stop. It is not for the one to (simply) suffice the other, as is the condition of some people. They believe in the shaykh's utmost perfection and think this belief should suffice them in attaing the goal. But they do not follow his example, nor carry out what he commands them to do, nor hold back from what he has forbidden them. So here are some of the statements of the knowledgeable of Allāh concerning the need (*ḍarūra*) for companionship and its benefits.

Ibn ʿAjība said in the Īqāẓ al-himam: "The shaykh of shaykhs Sīdī ʿAlī al-Jamal, may Allāh be pleased with him, said in his book that the best way for the student to arrive to Allāh the Exalted is by sitting with the knowledgeable one (*ʿārif*) of Allāh, if he can find him. Sitting with the gnostic is better than seclusion (*ʿuzla*), and seclusion is better than sitting with the heedless common folk, and sitting with the heedless is better than sitting with the ignorant disciple (*al-faqīr al-jāhil*). This is because the gnostic joins the aspirant with his Lord with a glance or with a word, while the ignorant disciple cuts him off from his Lord with a glance or a word. So there is nothing better than sitting with the gnostic."

The story of Prophet Moses (Mūsā), upon him peace, and Khiḍr is strong evidence of the need for companionship with a gnostic shaykh, the submission to him and the obedience to his command in order to obtain what is desired, Divine gnosis. The gnostic Amīr ʿAbd al-Qādir al-Jazāʾirī said in his book *al-Mawāqif*:

> Moses, upon him peace, whatever the greatness of his own capacity and the exaltedness of his affair, sought out the meeting with Khiḍr, upon him peace. He suffered aching longing and difficulty in his journey, as he said, "*Surely we have suffered much fatigue at this stage in our journey*" (Qurʾān, 18:62). With all of this, he was unable to bear with one interdiction, which was Khiḍr's saying, "*Do not ask me any questions until I speak to you about it*" (18:70). So Moses did not benefit from the knowledge of Khiḍr, even though Moses was absolutely certain that Khiḍr, by Allāh the Exalted's testimony, had more knowledge than him. When Moses said, "I do not know anyone more knowledgeable than I am," Allāh said, "Nay, with us is Khiḍr." For Moses did not specify one type of knowledge over another, his statement was a generalization.
>
> Moses in the beginning was not aware that he was unprepared to accept anything from the knowledge of Khiḍr. But Khiḍr knew this right away, so he said, "*You will not be able to have patience with me*" (18:67). Khiḍr, upon him peace, knew this from knowledgeable insight. Let the intelligent contemplate the exemplary conduct (*adab*) of these two masters.
>
> Moses, upon him peace, asked, "*May I follow you so that you may teach me of what you have learned?*" (18:66). In other words, "Can you give me permission to follow you, in order to learn from you?" Such words reflect the sweetness of exemplary conduct that those of sound spiritual experience have tasted.
>
> Khiḍr, upon him peace, said, "*If you should follow me,*

do not ask me any questions until I speak to you about it" (18:70). He did not say, "Do not ask me anything!" and then remain silent so that Moses would have remained confused and languishing. Rather he promised to speak to him about it, to explain the wisdom of what he did.

Ibn ʿAṭāʾ-Allāh Iskandarī, may Allāh be pleased with him, said in *Miftāḥ al-falāḥ*:

It is necessary for the one resolved on seeking guidance that he should follow the path of guidance, that he search out a shaykh among the folk of spiritual realization (*taḥqīq*). The one who walks this path leaves aside his passion. He plants his feet firmly in the service (*khidma*) of his master. When he finds him, he should implement what he commands and avoid what he forbids.

Ibn ʿAṭāʾ-Allāh also said in *Laṭāʾif al-minan*:

Your shaykh is not someone from whom you hear; your shaykh is someone from whom you receive. Your shaykh is not someone whose expressions confront you, your shaykh is the one whose signals become secreted within you. Your shaykh is not he who calls you to the door, but he who removes the veil between himself and you. Your shaykh is not the one whose words challenge you, but him whose spiritual state uplifts you. Your shaykh is the one who releases you from the prison of your vain desires and brings you into the Presence of the Lord. Your shaykh is the one who never ceases to polish the mirror of your heart, until the lights of your Lord become manifest therein. He will encourage you towards Allāh so that you will set off towards Him, and he will be with you until you arrive in His Presence. He will not cease to be by your side until he has cast you between His Hands and thrust you into the light of the Divine Presence. Then he will say, "Here you are and here is your Lord."

Ibn ʿAṭāʾ-Allāh also said, "Do not keep the company

of one whose spiritual state does not uplift you and whose words do not lead you towards Allāh."

The Proof of Islam, Imam Abū Ḥāmid al-Ghazālī, may Allāh have mercy on him, said:

> In the beginning of my affair, I used to deny the spiritual states of the righteous and the stations of the gnostics. Then I kept companionship with my shaykh (Yūsuf al-Nasāj). He did not cease polishing me with (the command to perform) strenuous exertions until I was favored with spiritual illuminations (*wāridāt*). I saw Allāh the Exalted in a dream. He said to me, "O Abū Ḥāmid! Put down your self-occupations. Keep companionship with the Sufi folk. I have put them in My satisfaction, and made them the locus of My gaze. They are those who have traded the two abodes for the love of Me." I said, "By Your Might! But what if I have less than good thoughts of them?" He said, "You have indeed (harbored such thoughts). What cuts you off from them is your being occupied with the love of the world. So leave aside the world in respect before you are forced out it in humiliation. I have poured on you lights from the holy assembly." Then I woke up in a happy state and went to my shaykh and related to him my dream. He smiled and said, "O Abū Ḥāmid, such are our elementary learning boards (*alwāḥ*) in the beginning. But companionship with me will beautify your vision with the luster of permanence."[6]

In his *Iḥyā ʿulūm al-dīn*, Imam al-Ghazālī also said:

> The aspirant requires a shaykh and teacher to emulate and to guide him to the balanced way. The way (*sabīl*) of religion is obscure (*ghāmiḍ*), and the ways of Satan are numerous and apparent. Who does not have a shaykh to guide him, Satan leads him to his paths. So who seeks the plain way of destruction with no sentinel, let him

---

6 This narration is excerpted from ʿAbd al-Bāqī Sarūr, *Shakhṣiyāt ṣūfiyya.*

ponder alone and destroy himself. The independent one (*mustaqil*) alone is like a tree that sprouts by itself, because it agitates the neighbors. Even if it remains long enough to grow leaves, it does not bear fruit. The aspirant must cling to his shaykh and hold tightly to him.

Someone offered these Divine pearls of wisdom:

> *There is no sweetness to life except the*
> *companionship of the Sufis (fuqarā')*
> *They are sultans, lords, and princes*
> *Sitting with them in companionship is to acquire*
> *proper comportment*
> *The dispensing of your fortune, no matter where you*
> *have been before.*

As for the question about seeking the shaykh, is it strictly incumbent (*farḍ*) on every single individual, or on some but not others, and what is the reason in either case? Our master, the Hidden Pole and the well-known Muḥammadan Seal Sīdī Aḥmad al-Tijani answered, as recorded in the book *Rawḍ al-muḥibb al-fānī* of Sīdī Muḥammad b. al-Mishrī:[7]

> The quest for the shaykh is not a duty imposed by the Sacred Law (*sharīʿa*), with the inevitable consequence of reward for its performance and punishment for its abandonment. There is nothing like that in the Shari'a, but it is obligatory from the perspective of common sense, just as the search for water is imperative for the thirsty person, for common sense tells him that he will perish if he doesn't find water to satisfy his thirst. Such a perspective relates to what has been mentioned, namely, human beings have only been created for the worship of Allāh and the sole dedication to the Divine Presence, by the rejection of everything besides Him.

7 This section is also comprises a portion of the eighth chapter of Shaykh Ibrāhīm Niasse's *Kāshif al-ilbās*.

The aspirant has come to know his own inability to make his lower self (*nafs*) to comply with the requirements of entering the Divine Presence, and has recognized the weakness of his own self in what is required to enter the Divine Presence in terms of fulfilling the necessary duties and proper modes of conduct (*adab*). He has come to know that he has no refuge or safety from Allāh if he should remain attached to his lower self, following its vain passions and turning away from Allāh the Exalted.

So from this perspective, it is clearly necessary for him to seek out the complete shaykh. This necessity is strictly a matter of natural logic, not a ruling derived from legal texts, since what is mentioned in the legal texts is only the obligation to fulfill the rights of Allāh, both inwardly and outwardly. This duty is an obligation on every single individual among His servants and no one has any legally valid excuse for neglecting it, nor has he any excuse for his subservience to vain desires and his inability to control his lower self. There is nothing in the Sacred Law except the incumbency thereof, and the penalty incurred by violating the prohibition of neglecting that duty. This is what is contained in the *Sharīʿa*. So the shaykh who must be sought after is the shaykh who is qualified to provide such instruction, he being the one who teaches the nature of the legal observances demanded of the servant, in terms of performance of the commandments and avoidance of the prohibitions.

Every person ignorant (of Allāh) must seek out the shaykh, for no one can do without him. Again, there is nothing other than this, from a legal perspective, that requires seeking out the shaykhs. But it is definitely an obligation from the perspective of common sense, since the ignorant person is comparable to the invalid. If such a person has resigned himself to sickness, on account of his inability to cure himself by his own means, one can only conclude that he wishes to remain sick. On the other hand, if the patient should demand how he may obtain perfect health, one would tell him to seek out the expert physician. Indeed, the expert physician is familiar with the sickness and its cause, he knows the medicine that will cure it and he knows how this medicine should be applied, how much should be taken, in what manner, how often, and under what circumstances. May Allāh's Peace be with you all.

The Comportment (adab) of the Perfected Actualized Gnostic Sages

The perfected shaykhs and the actualized gnostics are unanimously agreed that proper conduct (*adab*) on the path of Allāh's people is most important in every matter. *Adab* is the confluence of all good and piousness. They have stipulated that it is necessary to journey the way of *adab* in everything. Who does so arrives and finds communion. Who does not is cut off and dissociated. The entire Sufi path is (nothing but) proper comportment (*ādāb*). For every time there is a proper conduct, for every state a conduct, and every station a conduct.

The Prophet, Allāh's peace and blessing upon him, said, "My Lord trained me with the best conduct, and then commanded me to perfect good character."

Conduct (*adab*) is the refinement of ones outward and inward self, and when this happens, a person becomes "well-mannered" (*adīb*). Ibn ʿArabī, may Allāh be pleased with him, said, "All good is gathered in proper conduct."

Ibn ʿAṭā'-Allāh said, "Proper conduct means that you are occupied with commendable things." Someone asked him what he meant. He said: "It means that you practice proper conduct with Allāh, in private and in public. If you do this, you will become well mannered, even if you do not speak Arabic." Then he recited:

When we speak, what comes forth is only beauty
And if we remain silent what comes forth is only beauty.

There is no more excellent speech than what some of the Sufis have said concerning proper conduct. (They said) Proper conduct (*adab*) is when the servant behaves with correct behavior, outwardly and inwardly. His outward self complies with the Sacred Law (*sharīʿa*) and follows the Sunnah in word and deed. His inward self is in accord with the Reality (*al-ḥaqīqa*). He accepts and is pleased with what Allāh desires of him. He sees that all blessing on him is from Allāh the Exalted, whether it comes right away or is delayed. If it is immediate, this is the soul's attainment of what it loves right away. If it is delayed, this is indeed a type of detriment or calamity visited upon him because of his mistakes; but the blessing will return to him later on. By this expression, it is still a blessing. The possessor of such conduct is favored to only see blessing, which covers over any rancor. So he witnesses the blessing of Allāh the Exalted on him externally and internally.

In a *ḥadīth* on the authority of Muʿādh b. Jabal, may Allāh be pleased with him, the Prophet, Allāh's peace and blessing upon him, said: "Help Islam by having good character and beautiful comportment."

Anas b. Mālik, may Allāh be pleased with him, is reported to have said, "Having good conduct while performing an action is a sign of the action being accepted (by Allāh)."

ʿAbd-Allāh b. al-Mubārak, may Allāh be pleased with him, said, "Whoever is negligent of good conduct, is punished with being deprived of the Prophetic behavioral ideal (*sunan*). Whoever is negligent of the Sunnah, is punished with being deprived of the legal incumbencies (*farā'iḍ*). Whoever is negligent of the incumbencies, is punished with the deprivation of gnosis (*ma'rifa*)."

Dhū l-Nūn al-Miṣrī, may Allāh be pleased with him, said: "If the aspirant (*murīd*) turns away from good conduct, he is sent back to whence he came."

As for the proper conduct with the spiritual guide (*shaykh*), it is to have firm conviction concerning his completion (*kamāl*), and that he is among the folk of guidance and spiritual training, combining the Sacred Law (*sharī'a*) and the Reality (*ḥaqīqa*), rapture (*jadhb*) with wayfaring (*sulūk*). (And it is to know) that he is in the footsteps of the Prophet, Allāh's blessing and peace on him. Secondly, he must exalt him and guard his reverence in his absence as well as his presence. Spiritual training is by the love he has for him in his heart, and this love is the evidence of his truthfulness. Who is not truthful does not travel, even if he were to remain with the Shaykh for a thousand years. May Allāh have mercy on Sīdī Muḥammad Sharqī, who said, "Who is not truthful, sells nothing with his boisterous shouting. Who does not rectify himself, does not pass through any door."

As for the proper conduct with the brethren, it was Ibn 'Ajība who mentioned: "Guard their honor whether they are present or absent. Do not slander anyone, and do not belittle anyone. Do not say, 'The companions of Sīdī so-and-so are perfected, and the companions of Sīdī so-and-so are wanting.' Or, 'So-and-so is a gnostic and so-and-so is not.' Or, 'So-and-so is weak (in faith), and so-and-so is strong.' Anything of this nature is the essence of calumny, and this is forbidden (*ḥarām*) by consensus, especially in the case of the saints. Their flesh is deadly poison, just as is the flesh of the scholars and the righteous. The aspirant is warned against this blameworthy trait, and is warned to flee from its imprint as one would flee from the lion. Whoever is prone to this will never succeed. The saints are like the Prophets, and who differentiates between them restricts their goodness and denies their blessing. Some of the Sufis have said that whomever is exposed by the disciples cannot be consoled by the Shaykh, but whomever the Shaykh exposes is consoled by the disciples."

Part of good conduct with the brethren is also to offer counsel and fellowship, and to work with them according to the principle, "And cooperate together in piety and God-consciousness." The Shaykh of Islam, our master al-Ḥājj Ibrāhīm said (in *Rūḥ al-adab*):

> *O seeker! You must have good conduct*
> *It is indeed the door for every wayfarer.*

And he said in the same poem:

> *Conduct yourself properly externally and internally*
> *With this does one ascend to high positions.*

Bewilderment and Surrender

Here is found complete faith that does not depend on tradition (*taqlīd*) and which is not satisfied by derived evidence alone. This faith depends on illuminated vision by which is witnessed the eternal Divine Presence. Such a person witnesses this Presence in all of his actions, movements, and stillness.

Long ago, one of the distinguished folk said, "No one knows Allāh except that He makes Himself known to him. No one witnesses the Divine Oneness, unless the Divine Oneness is made witness to him. No one believes in Him except He is kind to him. No one is purified except Allāh manifests in his inner most being. No one is made sincere except Allāh attracts him to Him. No one is made righteous except Allāh creates this righteousness Himself."

And it is said that the creation is only able to describe the Creator with the tongue of incapacity, which is why the Prophet, Allāh's peace and blessing upon him, said, "I cannot enumerate the ways of praising You! You are as You have praised Yourself!" This was narrated in Muslim and in other ḥadīth collections.

It has been narrated by al-Tirmidhī in *Nawādir al-uṣūl*, "Allāh the Most High has concealed Himself from the faculties of the intellect (*ʿuqūl*), just as He concealed Himself from the eyes (*abṣār*), and the heavenly hosts seek Him just as you seek Him." This is why Junayd said, "The ending point of the intellect is bewilderment (*ḥayra*)." Dhū l-Nūn al-Miṣrī said, "The utmost degree of the gnostics is bewilderment."

Allāh the Exalted said, "*Allāh warns you all of Himself, and Allāh is Compassionate with His servants*" (3:30).

And He said, "*They have not given Allāh a just estimation of His power*" (22:74).

And He said, "*He knows what is before them and behind them, and they have not gauged the extent of His knowledge*" (20:110).

And He said, "*And they do understand the smallest fragment of His knowledge except as He wills*" (2:255).

And He said, "*Do not pursue that of which you have no knowledge. Indeed, the hearing, sight, and heart, will all be held to account*" (17:36).

And He said, "*Say, My Lord has only forbidden indecencies, such of them as are apparent and such as are hidden, and sin and wrongful oppression, that you associate with Allāh that for which He has not sent down authority, and that you say about Allāh that which you do not know*" (7:33).

And He said, "*Glorious is your Lord, the Lord of Might, above what they (falsely) attribute to Him*" (37:180).

All of this demonstrates that the created entities, whatever they are, cannot delimit the Creator. They cannot comprehend Him by expression, for His Essential Being (*dhāt*) is free from specification. The one who is able to comprehend Allāh is none but Allāh Himself, none other. Human minds are weak and limited, and cannot understand Divine Oneness (*tawḥīd*) and gnosis except that a created thing is in need of a creator. This is why Allāh has not overburdened the mind with the incumbency of understanding Him. It is enough that mankind submits and believes in Him. Imam al-Buṣayrī said:

He did not try us with things that baffle the mind
Such was his concern for us, so we neither doubted nor strayed

From all of this we understand that gnosis is an activity of the heart, not of the mind. This is why Abū Bakr al-Ṣaddīq, may Allāh be pleased with him, said, "The incapacity to attain realization is itself a realization." Also in this meaning, the consummate scholar Muḥammad Fāl wuld Matālī said:

Plunging into comprehending Him is associating partners with Him
The incapacity in comprehending Him is itself a realization
The incapacity in comprehending Him is (the station) of (Abū Bakr) the truthful
For he said this was itself the comprehension and the realization.

The Veil (al-ḥijāb)

The Prophet, peace and blessings of Allāh be upon him, said, "Allāh has 70,000 veils of light and darkness. If He were to remove them, the radiant splendor of His Countenance would burn up whomever His Gaze met." I would add that the folk of Allāh are in unanimous agreement that the "veils" are in relation to the servant, not the Real, Glorified and Exalted is He. The proof for this is the fact that nothing actually veils the Countenance of Allāh. He continually manifests Himself to the creation, with a manifestation that is direct and immediate, from the beginning of the act of creation, and nothing has been burned from that manifestation. So, were there veils for Him then the entire cosmos would have been burned with just one glance from Him, as mentioned in the *ḥadīth*. So understand well.

The "greatest Shaykh" Imam Muḥyi al-Dīn Ibn ʿArabī said in his book *al-Ḥujub*:

> O lover, whoever you are, know that the veils between you and your beloved, whomever it is, are nothing except your tarrying with (created) things, the things are not veils themselves. It is said to the one who has not "tasted" the flavor of the spiritual realities: you have tarried with created things because of the shortcoming of your perception. In other words: a lack of penetration,

> expressed by the term "veil" (*ḥijāb*). The veil itself is nonexistent, and in nonexistence (*al-ᶜadam*) there is no single thing, and no veil. If there were actually veils, whoever became veiled from you, would also have been veiled. As for the gnostic, for whom the Real has become his hearing and sight, this one knows what is meant by "veil".

Know that if you have become completely occupied with a matter, you necessarily have tarried with it. This stopping is your veil, for stopping with the creation veils you from the Real, while stopping with the Real veils you from the creation. This is the (difference between) extension (of the self into the world) and (Divine) intimacy, mentioned in the Qur'an and the Sunnah as darkness versus illuminated love. The veils become constructed on the basis of this worldly self-extension.

Ibn ᶜAjība said in *Īqāẓ al-Himam*: "The Real is not veiled from you, rather it is you who are veiled from seeing Him, for were there anything to veil Him, then that which veils Him would cover Him, and if He were covered then that would be a limitation to His Being, for if something contains something else, it overpowers it. '*And He is the Omnipotent, overpowering His servants*' (Qur'ān, 6:18).

I would add that veiling is inconceivable for the reality of the Real, exalted is He. Nothing veils Him. He is Manifest by everything, before everything, after everything. Nothing else is manifest with Him, and there is no existence in reality except for Him. He is not veiled from you, rather it is you who are veiled from seeing Him by your belief in otherness and the attachment of your heart to sensory affairs. If your heart were completely devoted to seeking the Lord, you would have refused to see anything else. You would have seen the Light of the Real shining brightly in the manifestations of being. What was veiled from you by fleeting illusions would have become witnessed directly.

In this meaning, Ibn ʿAṭāʾ-Allāh said, "The Real did not veil Himself from you by some reality coexisting with Him, since there is no reality other than Him. What veils you from Him is nothing but the illusion that something is existing with Him." One of the Sufi poets said:

You are not unveiled except by lifting the veil
What is extraordinary is that the appearance is
covered over in the first place.

Another poet said:

She appeared and is not hidden from anyone
Except the one born blind, unable to see the moon
But she hid herself with what appeared as a veil
How to know Him who became concealed by Might?

Ibn ʿAjība also said in the *Īqāẓ al-himam*: "The Most High became veiled in His state of appearance. This is evidence of the existence of his omnipotence, as was pointed out in the *Ḥikam* (of Ibn ʿAṭāʾ-Allāh) with the words, 'Among the evidences of the existence of His omnipotence (*qahr*), glorious is He, is that He veils you from Him with what has no existence with Him.'"

Allāh veiled Himself from the creation with things that do not exist. They are illusions, and illusions lack reality, they do not exist. What veils Him is the intensity of His appearance. And the vision is not prevented from seeing Him except by the overpowering nature of His Light. Allāh is alone in the existence, for there is nothing existing with Allāh.

The Most High said, "*Everything is perishing (hālik) except His Countenance*" (Qurʾān, 28:88). And the verbal noun (*hālik*) is in reality the expression of a permanent condition.

And the Most High said, "*He is the First, the Last, the Manifest, the Hidden*" (57:3).

And Allāh said, "*Wherever you turn, there is the Face of Allāh*" (2:115).

And Allāh said, "*He is with you wherever you are*" (57:4).

And Allāh said, "*We told you that your Lord is all around mankind*" (17:60).

And Allāh said, "*And you (Muḥammad) did not throw when you threw, but Allāh was He who threw*" (8:17).

And Allāh said, "*Surely those who pledged allegiance to you (Muḥammad), pledged allegiance to Allāh*" (48:10).

The Prophet, Allāh's blessing and peace on him, said, "The best words spoken by a poet were those of Labīd, "Surely everything other than Allāh is falsehood (*bāṭil*), and every (worldly) blessing is illusionary, perishing."

And the Prophet, Allāh's blessing and peace on him, said, "Allāh says, 'O My servants! I was sick and you did not visit Me.' They say, 'O Lord! How can we visit You, the Lord of the worlds?' Allāh says, 'When my servant so-and-so became ill, you did not visit him. If you had visited him you would have found Me with him.'" This ḥadīth is an indication that these (creations) are but skeletons, and people are phantoms without any reality belonging to themselves. They are like shadows.

Our master, the Shaykh of Islam, Shaykh Ibrāhīm Niasse quoted from Shaykh al-Tijānī in the book *Kāshif al-ilbās* to explain the removal of the veil.

> The removal of the veil is dependent on quickly detaching oneself from worldly desires, desisting from exalting their worth and hasty procurement of their benefits. Their harmful effects can be prevented by gracious and gentle asceticism (*zuhd*), rather than complete renunciation or abstinence. The causes of the veil consist of excessive eating, drinking, socializing, talking, sleeping and

> continual heedlessness of the remembrance of Allāh, Exalted is He. These causes are severed by hunger and thirst in gentle moderation, removing oneself from social mixing, persistent absolute silence except in rare cases of necessity, keeping the night vigil in gentle moderation, and constant remembrance of Allāh with the heart and tongue, unceasingly and with any form of remembrance. The types of remembrance that remove the veils include those that tear away the veil from the spirit completely and those that are partially effective, removing a veil of a particular kind. The remembrances which are totally effective are the following: *lā ilāha ill-Allāh* or *Ṣalāt ʿala l-Nabbī* or *Subḥān-Allāh* or *al-Ḥamdu li-Llāh* or *Allāhu Akbar* or *Bismi-Llāh al-Raḥmān al-Raḥīm* or *Allāh Allāh Allāh* or *Allāhu lā ilāha illa Huwa l-Ḥayy al-Qayyūm.* The remembrances that are partially effective include the rest of the Beautiful Names of Allāh. Each Name removes one type of veil, but does not apply to another. And the success is with Allāh, the Most High.

Shaykh Ibrāhīm said, "These words of his are worthy of being inscribed with golden ink! If someone wants more information on how to tear away the veils, in addition to what has been provided here, let him keep company with the distinguished experts on the subject." He continued:

> Sīdī al-ʿArabī b. al-Sāʾiḥ, may Allāh be pleased with him, said, "The *Jawāhir al-maʿānī* contains numerous methods, all of them leading to Allāh the Exalted." I would point out that more has been concealed than what has been made public. The Director of Fortune directs some people, while the Divine Averter misguides others. As one poet said: "The rain pours down and the earth becomes green, whether the seeker of goodness settles there or leaves."

Entering the Holy Presence

Ibn ʿAjība said: "The Divine Presence is sanctified and exalted, and no one enters it except the purified. It is prohibited for the impure heart to enter the Presence's mosque, and the filth of the heart is its heedless of its Lord."

"The Most High said: '*O you who believe, do not approach the prayer while you are intoxicated, until you know what you are saying, and [do not approach] while in a state of ritual impurity, except while traveling, until you have cleansed yourselves*' (4:43).

"In other words, do not approach worship in the Divine Presence while you are drunk with the love of the world and the witness of otherness, until you wake up and reflect on what you are saying in the Presence of the Sovereign Lord. And do not come with the filth of heedlessness and the witness of otherness until you are cleansed with the water of the unseen. Ibn ʿArabī al-Ḥātimī was referring to this when he said:

Purify yourself with the water of the unseen if you would possess a secret
If not, make the dry ablution (tayammum) with dust or stone
Put forth an Imam in front of you

And pray the dawn prayer in the beginning of its time

This is the prayer of the knowledgeable of their Lord
So if you are among them, come quench the dry land with the ocean.[8]

"In other words, purify yourself from the witness of your self (*nafs*) with the water of the unseen, the witness of your Lord. Or in other words, purify yourself from the witness of the senses to the witness of the meaning. Or, purify yourself from seeing the seen world with the water of seeing the unseen world. Or, purify yourself from the witness of otherness with the water of knowledge of Allāh. He is surely hidden from you by everything other than Him, but if you cleanse yourself from the witness of otherness, you will have cleansed yourself from all defects."

Some time ago, I wrote the following verses similar to this in meaning:

I found my goal after the denial of everything other than Him
He is the One, the Near to all of His creation

There is nothing besides the Real in every single place
So let the one desiring arrival contemplate the achievement of his arrival.

---

8 These verses are sometimes also attributed to Junayd al-Baghdadi. An alternative recording of these verses to the one included here reads, "Perform the ablution" instead of "purify yourself", and "pray the midday prayer" instead of "pray the dawn prayer."

Qur'an Verses and Prophetic Statements explaining Gnosis

The Most High said: "*Allāh is the Light of the heavens and the earth. The simultude of His light is as a niche wherein is a lamp. The lamp is in a glass, the glass, is as it were a glittering star, lighted from a blessed tree, an olive, neither of the east, nor of the west, whose oil would almost glow forth, even if no fire touched it. It is light upon light. Allāh guides whom He will to His light; and Allāh sets forth parables to mankind, for Allāh is knower of all things.*

In the houses which Allāh has allowed to be raised up, that His Name may therein be remembered. In them is He glorified morning and evening.

People whom neither merchandise nor sale distract them from the remembrance of Allāh, and from the observance of prayer, and paying to the poor their due. This because they fear a day when hearts and eyes will be overturned.

That Allāh may recompense them for the best of what they did, and increase the reward for them of His bounty. Allāh provides for whom He wills without measure."[9]

Allāh has here explained the reality that He has a general, comprehensive light (*nūr ʿām*) by which He has

9 Qur'an, 24:35-38. The translation here is that of Ali Özek, *The Glorious Qur'an* (Istanbul: Asyr Media, 1995).

illuminated the heavens and earth.[10] By this light existence (*wujūd*) was manifested from a state of non-manifestation. (The emphasis on light is appropriate because) the idea that the manifestation of something by something else is in effect a claim of existence for the thing manifested in and of itself. Allāh is the Manifest by His Essential Being, the manifestation of other than Him is the Light. So He is the Light that manifested the heavens and the earth by His shining upon them. But where sensory lights make dense bodies appear to the senses by shining upon them, the manifestation of things from the Divine Light is different. The Divine Light is the essence of their existence, whereas the sensory light's illumination of dense bodies does not mean that it is the source of their existence.

There is also a special light (*nūr khāṣṣ*) by which He enlightens the believers and guides them to Him through their righteous deeds. That is the light of gnosis (*maʿrifa*) by which He enlightens their hearts and their vision (on) "*a day when hearts and eyes will be overturned.*" So they are guided by this light to their eternal happiness. In this light they witness with their eyes what had been hidden from them in the material world (*dunyā*). The Most High compared this light to a lamp inside of a glass inside of a niche, lit from an oil of utmost purity. The glass gleams as if it were a glittering star. So light is added upon light. The lamp is placed in the houses of worship, in which Allāh is glorified by believers who are not distracted from the remembrance and worship of their Lord by buying and selling.

This is a description of how Allāh has honored the believers, those in pursuit of eternal happiness, with the light of knowing Him. He has forbidden the deniers (*kāfirūn*)

---

10 The text of the speech begins this sentence with "Some of those of knowledge have said…", but this has been dispensed for the sake of readability and because the text that follows does not appear to be a direct citation.

from this light, and left them in the darkness where they cannot see. So Allāh has favored whoever occupies himself with his Lord, who turns away from the exhibition of the life of this world through a light from His presence. And Allāh does what He wills. To Him belong the sovereignty and the final destination.

Concerning the words of the Most High, "*And they have not appraised of Allāh a true appraisal*" (6:91), al-Akhfash[11] said: "It means they have not known Him with true gnosis."

Consider the words of the Messenger, Allāh's peace and blessing upon him: "Who knows himself, knows his Lord." Muḥyī al-Dīn Ibn ʿArabī said on the basis of this ḥadīth: "He, the peace and blessing of Allāh on him, was pointing out with these words that you are not you. Rather, you are Him in the negation (*bilā*) of you. He is not inside you, nor is He removed from you. And you are not removed from Him, nor are you inside of Him. This does not mean that you exist, or that your description is fixed by sufficiency in Him. Since you were once nothing, you are not presently anything, not by your own self, not in Him, not with Him. You are neither passing out of existence, nor do you exist. You are He, and He is you, without any reason to explain. If you have come to know that your existence is defined like this, you have come to know Allāh. If not, then not."

The Prophet, Allāh's peace and blessing upon him, said on the authority of ʿĀʾisha, may Allāh be pleased with her: "The support of the house is its foundation. The support of the religion is the knowledge (*maʿrifa*) of Allāh the Most High, certainty, and the restrained mind." (He was asked) "What is the restrained mind?" He said, "The cessation from the disobedience to Allāh, and guarding the obedience to

---

11 This is likely ʿAbd al-Ḥamīd al-Akhfash al-Akbar (d. 793 C.E.), a famous Arabic grammarian who lived in Basra, Iraq.

Allāh."[12] The Prophet also said, "Who is pleased with Allāh as his Lord, Islam as his religion, and Muḥammad, Allāh's blessing and peace on him, as his Prophet, has tasted (*dhāq*) the sweetness of faith."[13] One poet said:

A sun rose from a most beloved night
Illuminating what was hidden
The sun of daylight is obscured by the night
But the sun of the hearts is never absent.

Another poet said:

Say "Allah" and cast aside the creation, and everything else
If you desire the attainment of perfection
Realize that everything besides Allah
Does not exist, whatever its particularization and beauty.[14]

A gnostic said:

I saw my Lord with the eye of my heart
So I said, there is no doubt You are You.

Another poet said:

When I saw Allāh I did not see anything other
With us, otherness is forbidden.

---

12 Hadith related by Imam Daylami.

13 The word "taste" (dhawq) is the same used by Sufis to describe the necessity of "tasting," or direct experience, of spiritual realities.

14 These verses are attributed to Abu Madyan (d. 1198) of Tlemcen (modern Algeria).

The Claim of the Cessation of Spiritual Training in the earlier generations and the Response of the Ṣāḥib al-Fayḍa

The allegations that spiritual training has been truncated in our time are nothing new. Some said the same in previous times, and some still repeat the claim despite the conclusive proofs with which our scholars have refuted their claims. Some even go so far as to claim the cessation of sainthood, and other things besides. Our master the Shaykh of Islam, the bringer of the Tijānī flood, Shaykh Ibrāhīm b. al-Ḥājj ʿAbd-Allāh Niasse spoke about this issue in his book, *Kāshif al-ilbās*. We will include the gist of his words on the subject here:[15]

According to Sidi (Aḥmad) Zarrūq,[16] in the book *Ta'sīs al-Qawā'id*: "Our Shaykh Abū al-'Abbās al-Ḥaḍramī said: 'spiritual training (*tarbiya*) in the technical sense has ceased to be practiced, and all that remains is training by

15 The following section is excerpted from Shaykh Ibrāhīm Niasse, *The Removal of Confusion Concerning the Flood of the Saint Seal Aḥmad al-Tijani* (Fons Vitae, 2010), 1-16.

16 Sidi Aḥmad Zarrūq al-Burnusi al-Fasi (d. 1493) was a North African scholarly Sufi of the Shādhilī order.

spiritual zeal (*himma*) and state (*ḥāl*). So it is incumbent on you to follow the Qur'ān and the Sunnah, without addition or subtraction.'" The rest of this quotation will be presented later. But let us say here that this statement, made in the ninth century after the Hijra (sixteenth century of the Common Era), should not be understood, especially by the one deprived of spiritual experience and gnosis, as meaning that spiritual training has ceased absolutely. Neither Zarrūq nor his Shaykh al-Ḥaḍramī meant this.

The actual meaning intended was explained by the erudite scholar Ibn 'Ajība in his *Īqāẓ al-Himam*:

> Some might hold to the literal meaning of al-Ḥaḍramī's words: "spiritual training in the technical sense has ceased to be practiced, and all that remains is training by spiritual zeal and state. So it is incumbent on you to follow the Qur'ān and the Sunnah." My response to this is as follows: Al-Ḥaḍramī did not mean to say that the cessation of spiritual training will last for all eternity. Far be it from al-Ḥaḍramī to pass such judgment on Allāh and limit His Power! What he meant was that there were many impostors and pretenders in his time, so he warned his contemporaries to beware of them. The high erudition of al-Ḥaḍramī and Zarrūq is inconsistent with the literal meaning of their words. Even if they are held to the literal meaning, that spiritual training had ceased for all eternity, they are surely not infallible. Every statement, theirs included, is subject to evaluation, except for the statement of our Prophet, Allāh's blessing and peace on him. Indeed, following the time of al-Ḥaḍramī, an innumerable number of distinguished Sufi scholars have been carrying out orthodox spiritual training by means of spiritual states (*ḥāl*), spoken words (*maqāl*), and zeal (*himma*). They also exist in this time of ours, famous like radiant beacons. Allāh has guided many of the creation with their assistance, and with their help He has taught the saints what no one knows, except those whom Allāh has blessed.

Ibn 'Ajība's explanation is proven by the appearance of Shaykh Aḥmad al-Tijānī, the Seal of Saints and the standard-bearer of spiritual training well after the ninth-century statements of al-Ḥaḍramī and his student. Shaykh al-Tijānī's role as a spiritual trainer cannot be doubted by anyone endowed with the slightest faith in and submission to him. The same is true of Shaykh al-Sayyid al-Mukhtār al-Kuntī,[17] as well as the perfected ones who were trained by such men, and thereby attained to the highest rank of those shaykhs providing spiritual training (*tarbiya*) and elevation (*tarqiya*). Our Shaykh and means of access to our Lord, Shaykh Aḥmad al-Tijānī, Seal of the Saints, may Allāh be pleased with him, has demonstrated that among the people of his spiritual Path are the masters of spiritual training (*mashā'ikh al-tarbiya*). This is indicated by his authentic statements recorded in the *Jāmi'*:[18]

> (He said) "If Allāh grants illumination (*fatḥ*) to my companions, the one among them who sits in my presence, in the town where I am, will fear his own destruction (*halāk*)." One of his companions asked him, "Is this from you, or from Allāh?" To this he replied, "It is from Allāh, without my having a choice in the matter." He mentioned this on the second Sunday of the sacred month of Sha'ban, in the year 1223 of the Hijra (1808 C.E.). Then he said on the next Monday: "The fear that was mentioned is for the one among my companions who has been authorized with the power of Divine disposition (*taṣarruf*), and to provide his fellow creatures with spiritual training (*tarbiya*)."

---

17 Al-Mukhtār al-Kuntī (d. 1811) lived near Timbuktu, Mali, and revived the Qadiriyya in West Africa.

18 The *Kitāb al-Jāmi' li al-'Ulūm al-Fā'ida min Biḥār al-Quṭb al-Maktūm* is one of the primary sources of the Tijānī order, written during the founder's lifetime in 1808 by Muḥammad b. al-Mishrī.

The complete statement of Sidi Zarrūq in *Ta'sīs al-Qawā'id* partially quoted earlier reads as follows:

> We conclude with the statement of our Shaykh Abū al-'Abbās al-Ḥaḍramī: "spiritual training (*tarbiya*) in the technical sense has ceased to be practiced, and all that remains is training by spiritual zeal (*himma*) and state (*ḥāl*). So it is incumbent on you to follow the Qur'ān and the Sunnah, without addition or subtraction. This applies to one's dealing with the Real (*al-Ḥaqq*), with one's own self (*nafs*), and with the creation.
>
> "Three things must be observed in one's relationship to the Real: the performance of obligatory duties, the avoidance of forbidden things, and the submission to the rule of the Sacred Law.
>
> "Three things also must be observed in dealing with one's ego-self (*nafs*): moderation, refraining from exciting it, guarding against its mischievous impulses toward (arbitrary) attraction and repulsion, acceptance and rejection, approach and retreat.
>
> "There are also three things to observe in one's relationship with the creation: providing their rightful dues, withholding oneself from their possessions, and eschewing that which disturbs their hearts, except in the unavoidable case of genuine necessity.
>
> "The aspirant (*murīd*) is doomed to destruction and failure if he should manifest any of the following: ostentation; a desire to influence the general administration of affairs; taking it on himself to correct the reprehensible behavior of the general public; preoccupation with Holy War (*jihād*), while neglecting other virtues; wanting to monopolize all merits for himself; seeking out the imperfections of his fellow brothers; preoccupation with warning others; acting on hearsay; participating in social gatherings with neither the intention to learn nor to teach; mixing with worldly leaders under the pretext of religious devotion; preoccupation with subtle intricacies (of the religion), rather than actual practice to rectify his faults; undertaking spiritual training (*tarbiya*) without

authorization (*taqdīm*) from a shaykh, imam or scholar; following any and every person, the one speaking truth and the one speaking falsehood, without distinguishing their spiritual states; looking down on those connected to Allāh, and assuming their insincerity because of what he sees in them; fondness for special permissions and ambiguous interpretations; preferring the esoteric (*bāṭin*) to the apparent (*ẓāhir*), or remaining content with the apparent without reference to the esoteric, or concluding something from one incompatible with the other; being satisfied with knowledge without practice, or practice without knowledge or reference to the spiritual state (*ḥāl*), or spiritual state without knowledge or practice; non-substantiation of his knowledge, practice, spiritual state or religious conviction in the sources of the Muslim community, such as the books of Ibn 'Aṭā' Allāh concerning esoteric knowledge, especially the *Tanwīr*,[19] or the *Madkhal* of Ibn al-Ḥājj[20] concerning exoteric knowledge, or the book of his Shaykh Ibn Abī Jamra,[21] and the works of the scholars who followed them. But if such an aspirant accepts the teachings of these authorities, he will be saved as a Muslim, if Allāh wills. Virtuousness and success are from Allāh.

"Allāh's Messenger, the blessing and peace of Allāh on him, was asked about the verse of the Qur'ān: '*O you who believe! Guard your own souls!*' (5:105). He replied, 'When you see greedy lust being obeyed, passionate desire being pursued, and every holder of an opinion

---

19 Ibn 'Aṭā' Allāh al-Iskandarī (d. 1309), *Kitāb al-Tanwīr fī Isāt al-Tadbīr* has been described as the "basic training manual for Sufis in North Africa." It has been translated by Scott Kugle, *The Book of Illumination* (Fons Vitae, 2005).

20 Muḥammad b. al-Ḥājj al-Abdari al-Fasi (d. 1336) taught at the Qayrawin University in Fes, Morocco, but traveled throughout North Africa and is buried in Egypt. His work, *Madkhal al-Shara al-Sharīf 'ala al-Madhāhib* is a four volume work discussing various points of Islamic law.

21 Ibn Abī Jamra (d. 1300) was a renowned Ḥadīth scholar and jurist of the Maliki school, originally from Andalusia but who settled in Cairo. His major work was *Bahjat al-Nufūs*, which is a commentary on *Ṣaḥīḥ Bukhārī*.

taking conceited pride in his opinion; be on special guard for your own soul (*nafs*)'[22] He also related a statement from the Scrolls of Abraham (*ṣuḥuf Ibrāhīm*): 'The intelligent person should be aware of his age (*zaman*), hold his tongue and mind his business. The intelligent one should also hold on to four times: a time in which he calls himself to account; a time he confides in his Lord; a time he spends with his brothers, the ones who make him aware of his faults and guide him toward his Lord; and a time in which he allows himself to enjoy permissible desires.'

"May Allāh provide us with this and help us in it. May He enable us and our companions to benefit thereby, for we are helpless without Him! He is sufficient for us, an excellent Custodian. May Allāh bless our master, Prophet and patron, Muḥammad, and peace upon his family and companions."

Careful study of Shaykh Abū al-'Abbās al-Ḥaḍramī's above statement reveals its true meaning. This is why the gnostic of Allāh, al-Sayyid al-'Arabī b. al-Sā'iḥ explained:

> The meaning of spiritual training (*tarbiya*) in this context (alluded to by Zarrūq) is spiritual training in the technical sense, which was developed after the first three centuries (following the Prophet). This is the spiritual training which Shaykh Zarrūq believed, on the authority of some of his masters, had ceased to be practiced. He was followed in this regard by the scholarly researcher al-Yūsī,[23] may Allāh have mercy on him, who said: "In the opinion of al-Ḥaḍramī and Zarrūq, the meaning was not that spiritual training has ceased in the sense of providing guidance based on the Qur'ān and the Sunnah, and the teaching of remembrance (*dhikr*). Nor did it mean the end of removing falsehood from the soul, ridding it of

22 Reported by Abū Dāwūd in his *Sunan*, by Imam al-Tirmidhī in his *Sunan*, and by Ibn Mājah in his *Sunan*.

23 Abū 'Alī al-Hassan b. Mas'ud al-Yusi (d. 1691) was a Moroccan scholar of the Nāṣiriyya Sufi order.

attachments and obstacles, with the support and spiritual zeal of the shaykh. Indeed, this (role of the shaykh) is by the permission he receives in his innermost being from the Presence of Allāh, or the Presence of His Messenger, either in a state of wakefulness or sleep. Far be it from the people of Allāh to think (such training has ceased)!" For more on this subject, consult al-Dhahab al-Ibrīz.[24]

There are several Qur'ānic verses and Prophetic traditions that contain indications and glad tidings concerning this group (*ṭā'ifa*) manifestly committed to the Truth. And they are not limited to a particular time or place. For example, Allāh the Exalted said: "*And among those whom We have created there is a community who guide with the Truth and establish justice therewith*" (Qur'ān, 7:181). In his marginal commentary on the *Jalālayn*, the scholarly gnostic, Shaykh Sidi al-Ṣāwī[25] said of this verse: "They are the community of Muḥammad, Allāh's peace and blessing on him, since in a Prophetic tradition he said: 'A group from my community will not cease being committed to the Truth, until Allāh's (final) command arrives.'"[26] Mu'āwiya once said while delivering a sermon: "I once heard Allāh's Messenger say, 'Among my community there will never cease being a group obedient to Allāh's command. They will not be harmed by those who forsake or oppose them, until Allāh's (final) command arrives while they are committed to this.'"[27]

This group is not limited to any particular time, or to

24 *Al-Dhahab* al-Ibrīz was written in 1720 by the disciple of the Shadhili Sufi, Shaykh 'Abd al-'Azīz al-Dabbāgh (d. 1717, Fes), Aḥmad al-Lamati.

25 Aḥmad al-Ṣāwī (d. 1825) was an important Indian scholar of the Maliki school of jurisprudence (*madhhab*) who wrote a commentary (*ḥāshiya*) on the *Tafsīr al-Jalālayn* of Jalāl al-Dīn al-Suyūṭī and Jalāl al-Dīn al-Maḥallī.

26 Reported by Imam al-Bukhārī in his *Ṣaḥīḥ*, by Imam Muslim in his *Ṣaḥīḥ*, by Abū Dāwūd in his *Sunan*, by al-Tirmidhī in his *Sunan*, and by Aḥmad b. Hanbal in his *Musnad*.

27 Ḥadīth reported in the collections of Muslim and Abū Dāwūd.

any particular location. Indeed, they are present in every place and time, for Islam always will be raised high and never be surpassed. The wanton sinners and purveyors of evil, however many they are, bear no consequence (on the ascendency of Islam). This is glad-tidings for the community of Muḥammad, making it known that Islam and the Muslims are endowed with sublimity and honor until the Day of Resurrection draws near. At this point, the bearers of the Qur'ān and the religious scholars will die. The Qur'ān will be erased from the books. The gentle wind will blow, and all in whom there is a tiny speck of faith with die. And this will not happen until after the (return and) death of Jesus, peace be upon him. Jesus will not die until after he slays the Antichrist (*al-Dajjāl*) and lives for forty years, as the Prophetic traditions have repeatedly confirmed. The Antichrist will not come until seven years after the (coming of) the Mahdī, at the head of a (new) century.

One narration reports the Prophet's words: "There will always be a group in the West (*al-Maghrib*) ..."[28] Muḥyī al-Dīn Ibn al-'Arabī al-Ḥātimī explained, "Allāh placed the station of the Seal (*al-khatmiyya*) and Concealment (*al-katmiyya*) in Morocco (*al-Maghrib*), for that is the place of secrets and concealment." For more on this, consult Ibn al-'Arabī's *al-Futūḥāt* (*al-Makkiyya*) and his *'Anqā' Mughrib fī Khatm al-Awliyā' wa shams al-Maghrib*. See also the *Bughyat* (*al-Mustafīd* of Muḥammad al-'Arabī b. al-Sā'iḥ).

Allāh the Exalted has said: "*A multitude from the earlier generations, and a multitude from the later generations*"

28 The full version of this Ḥadīth, found in *Ṣaḥīḥ Muslim* on the authority of Abū Hurayra: "The people of the West (*al-Maghrib*) will remain manifestly committed to the Truth, they will not be harmed by those who go against them or forsake them until the Final Hour." Imam Aḥmad b. Hanbal considered this to refer to the people of Shām (Syria), but other scholars considered this to refer to North Africa, as *al-Maghrib* is the Arabic name for Morocco. Certainly this latter opinion was held by Ibn al-'Arabī.

(Qur'ān, 56:39-40). Ibn 'Abbās reported that Allāh's Messenger, Allāh's blessing and peace on him, said: "The two multitudes are from my community."[29] This is found in *al-Jawāhir al-Ḥisān*.[30] According to Shihāb al-Dīn al-Khafājī in *Nasīm al-Riyāḍ*:[31]

> The Prophet's saying, "The best of you are my generation, then those who will follow them, then those who will follow them,"[32] is not inconsistent with his saying, "My community is like the rain, for it is not known whether the best is in its first part or in its last." [33] The first part comes in one valley, and the last comes in another; meaning that somebody may come in this community (of Muḥammad) who provides people with tremendous benefit, beyond the means of anyone who preceded him. The first rain refers to particular individuals (from the earlier generations), while the second rain refers to the complete span of time (comprising the later generations); and indeed, what a difference there is between the two (for individuals to equal the whole span of time)!

Shaykh Zarrūq, may Allāh be pleased with him, said in *Ta'sīs al-Qawā'id*:

> The preferential regard for certain times and people is a vestige of pagan ignorance and has no legal foundation.

---

29 Reported by Imam Ibn Jarīr al-Ṭabarī in his *Tafsīr*, and cited by Imam al-Haythami in *Majma' al-Zawā'id wa Mamba' al-Fawā'id.*

30 This is the multi-volume Qur'ān exegesis, *Jawāhir al-Ḥisān fī Tafsīr al-Qur'ān*, by Abd al-Raḥmān al-Tha'alibi (d. 1471).

31 This is the *Nasīm al-Riyāḍ fī sharḥ Shifā' al-Qāḍī Īyād*, a commentary on the *Shifā'* of Qadi Iyad (work of Ḥadīth and Prophetic biography from the 12th century) by the Egyptian Hanafi scholar Shihāb al-Dīn al-Khafājī (d. 1659).

32 Reported by al-Bukhārī in his *Ṣaḥīḥ*, by Imam Muslim in his *Ṣaḥīḥ*, by al-Nasā'ī in his *Sunan*, by Aḥmad in his *Musnad*, by al-Ṭaḥāwī in *Sharḥ Ma'āni al-Āthār*, and by al-Ṭabarānī in *al-Mu'jam al-Kabīr*.

33 Reported by al-Tirmidhī in his *Sunan* and by Aḥmad b. Hanbal in his *Musnad*.

Thus the unbelievers said, "*If only this Qur'ān had been revealed to some great man from the two towns*" (Qur'ān, 43:31)![34] So Allāh the Exalted responded to them with His saying, "*Are they the ones who apportion the mercy of your Lord*" (43:32)? And when they said, "*We found our fathers following a religion, and we are guided by their footprints*" (43:22), Allāh responded to them by saying, "(The one sent to warn them) said: '*What, even though I bring you better guidance than what you found your fathers following*'" (43:24)?

It is necessary to consider the universality of Allāh's gracious favor (*faḍl*), without regard for a certain time or an individual, except in the case of someone specifically distinguished by the Word of the Most High. In this respect (of being distinguished by Allāh), the saints followed the Prophets; for the saintly miracle (*karāma*) bears witness to the Prophetic miracle (*mu'jiza*), and the scholars are the heirs of the Prophets in sanctity and mercy. Nonetheless, they are differentiated by the extent of their endowment with Divine grace (*faḍl*), so understand this well.

Concerning Allāh's saying, "*And a multitude from the later generations (are among the companions of the Right)*" (56:40), our Shaykh (al-Tijānī), our means of access, the nourishment of our spirits, our supporter, the saintly pole (*quṭb*), the succor (*ghawth*), the Seal of Muḥammadan sainthood (*al-khatim al-Muḥammadī*), said: "They are our companions!" Consider this fairly, and you will find that Shaykh al-Tijānī acquired the complete inheritance (of the Prophet), so that the two multitudes came to be in the Muslim community. One multitude belongs to his grandfather, they being the companions of the Allāh's Messenger, the peace and blessing of Allāh on him. The other multitude belongs to him, may Allāh be pleased with him, they being his own

34 The "two towns" refered to here are the main cities of Arabia at the time: Mecca and Yathrib (later called Medina).

companions. My pen recoils from inscribing the rest of the implications here.

In the secret of secrets are subtle details
If we were to reveal them, our blood would be shed publicly.

Know that not even those with the lowest degree of faith can maintain the cessation of the Prophet's spiritual support (*madad*), or the waning of the light of his Prophecy. Our Shaykh (al-Tijānī) said, as recording in *al-Jāmi*ᶜ and *al-Jawāhir* (*al-Ma*ᶜ*ānī*):[35]

> Know that the Prophet, Allāh's blessing and peace on him, used to impose general rules on the general populace (*al-ʿāma*) during his lifetime. Thus when he declared something unlawful, it became unlawful for everybody. When he prescribed something, he prescribed it for everybody. This was the case for all the manifest rulings of the Sacred Law.
>
> In addition to all of these general rulings, he used to instruct the elite (*al-khāṣṣa*) with special knowledge (*khāṣṣa*), and he used to single out certain of his companions and not others for certain affairs. This is something well-known and thoroughly recorded in the traditional reports concerning him.
>
> When he was transferred to the abode of the Hereafter, the situation was therefore the same as it had been during his life in this world. He had begun to entrust to his community the special command for the elite, but without modification of the general command given to everybody. So modification of the general command ceased with his death, while the flood of his grace (*fayḍahu*) persisted in providing the special command to the elite.

35 The *Jawāhir al-Ma'ānī wa bulūgh al-amānī fī fayḍ Sidi Abī al-ʿAbbās al-Tijānī* was written in 1799 by ʿAlī Harāzim al-Barāda, the closest companion of Shaykh Aḥmad al-Tijānī. The work is considered the most important primary source of the Tijāniyya.

Whoever imagines that all of his support for his community came to an end with his death, as in the case of other dead men, he is ignorant of the Prophet's rank. He is guilty of treating him indecently, and he is therefore in danger of dying as an unbeliever if he does not repent of his deluded conviction.

The Tijānī Sufi path and the Way of Gnosis

The goal of the Sufi path (*ṭarīqa*) of Sīdī Aḥmad al-Tijānī, may Allāh be pleased with him, is, as with other Sufi paths, the connection of the aspirant to Allāh, Blessed and Exalted. Its goal is to take him by the hand for the duration of his journey until he enters the Divine Presence. That is the assiduous desire of every path. The *Ṭarīqa Aḥmadiyya Muḥammadiyya Tijāniyya* is distinguished from other paths by the plethora of blessing (*barakāt*), the power of its radiating lights, and the persistence of its luminosity. How could this not be so, when it is the path of the Seal of Saints? How excellent the glad tidings and spiritual provisions that have been enfolded in this path! And our information about this path comes from what the Messenger of Allāh, the peace and blessing of Allāh on him, himself informed our master Abū ʿAbbās (Aḥmad al-Tijānī), may Allāh be pleased with him.

After this honor, there gushed forth the Tijānī gnosis, a flood from its wells on the hand of its possessor (Shaykh Ibrāhīm Niasse), may Allāh be pleased with him. So people hastened to him and accepted him, and entered group upon group into this Sufi path at his hand. Even his previous enemies confessed that this was the possessor of the flood of gnosis (*ṣāḥib al-fayḍa*) that had been foretold. As the true owner of the flood, he gave spiritual training and elevation, and dispensed annihilation and persistence (in the Divine presence). He purified people and cleansed them, until all of them entered the presence of devotional worship and they came to stand before their Lord. That was his aspiration and work. He himself said: "As for my fellow travelers, my aim with them is to quench their thirst in the presence of Allāh, the Generous Lord."

Thus it was that his brother, himself a most knowledgeable scholar, praised Shaykh Ibrāhīm in a poem:

> *He repaired the Path of our Shaykh al-Tijānī*
> *In our country, when the structures had collapsed*
> *He restored the Path of our Hidden Shaykh*
> *After it had been sold for properties and chattels*
> *He rebuilt the Path's edifice that had fallen into disrepair*
> *Floundering in desolation, including religious knowledge (ʿilm).*[36]

This (restoration) was because Shaykh Ibrāhīm cleaned the Tijāniyya Sufi path from all defects and innovation. He defended it from the prejudiced people, those misguided and misguiding others. He laid out a clear path for spiritual training, and who walks it arrives without trouble. The Shaykh said about this *Ṭarīqa*:

> The implementation of the litany (*wird*) of this *Ṭarīqa* by itself trains (the aspirant in gnosis). This is because he combines the plea for forgiveness (*istighfār*), prayer upon

36 These verses were authored by Shaykh Ibrāhīm's older brother, Muḥammad "Zaynab" Niasse, and were included in the first comprehensive biography of Shaykh Ibrāhīm written by Saydī ʿAlī Cissé for the publication of the *Kāshif al-ilbās* in 1935.

> the Prophet (*ṣalāt ʿala-l-nabbī*), and the remembrance of Allāh's Oneness (*haylala*, saying *lā ilāha ill-Allāh*). The meaning of the plea for forgiveness is removing oneself from sins and depravities. Prayer on the Prophet is to become endowed with excellent merits. The remembrance of Allāh's Oneness is to witness the Divine manifestation, where Allāh the Blessed and Exalted may manifest on the tongue of His servant with His words (in the Qurʾān), "*There is no god but Him*" (2:255), or "*There is no god but You*" (21:87), or "*There is no god but I*" (2:186).

If you look into these words, you will know that they cannot emerge except from a realized gnostic and most accomplished scholar, may Allāh be pleased with him.

The *Kāshif al-ilbās* of Shaykh Ibrāhīm Niasse contains a detailed exposition, quite sufficient for our purposes, of spiritual training in our Sufi path. The Shaykh said:

> The sphere of spiritual training (*tarbiya*) revolves around two poles. The first is the establishment of the five ritual prayers in accordance with their proper conditions. The second is the invocation of blessing on the Prophet throughout the night and at the beginning and end of the day, with the intention of obeying Allāh's command to do so; and this with magnification, reverence and love (for the Prophet). This follows the strict observance of the obligatory daily litany (*wird*), which confirms the authenticity of being a Tijānī aspirant.
>
> In the *Bughyat* (*al-Mustafid*), one of the main books of the Tijānī path, the illustrious spiritual master and venerable guide, the father of endowments, al-Sayyid 'Arabi b. Sā'iḥ, said on the subject of spiritual training:
> "The sphere of spiritual training and purification in this noble Muḥammad path of ours is centered on five practices. The first is the obligatory daily litany, without which entry into this path is invalid whatever a person's scholarly credentials. The second practice,

linked to the first, is the attendance of the congregational remembrance; both the daily office (*waẓīfa*) and the weekly remembrance of "there is no god but Allāh" (*haylala*) following the afternoon prayer on Friday.

"The next essential practice is the attendance of the five daily ritual prayers. Certainly all the practices mentioned here require careful observance of the stipulated conditions and proper modes of conduct in order to attain excellence and perfection. But of all the practices, the most imperative is the careful observance of the five daily prayers with their traditional elements as prescribed by the Sacred Law. You must comply with these stipulations as much as possible, perfectly fulfilling the basic elements of the prayer as established by customary practice.

"The next step in spiritual training is the aspirant's dedication to the invocation of blessing on the Prophet (*ṣalāt 'ala al-nabiyy*) to the maximum extent possible, in all available moments. The best method thereof is with the Invocation of Opening what was Locked (*ṣalāt al-fātiḥ lima ughliq*), which is one of the most exalted and precious treasures.

"Lastly, the aspirant undergoing spiritual training must persist in loving affection for the Prophet and gratitude to Allāh the Most High. He should rely only on Divine grace, the sole means of realizing sainthood. In this way, sainthood is realized without the necessity of secluded retreat (*khalwa*), excessive strenuous exertion, or any of the other methods of training adopted after the earliest centuries of Islam.

"The type of spiritual path described here is what our master (Shaykh Aḥmad al-Tijānī) was commanded to follow by the master of existence, the fountain of spiritual assistance and generosity, Allāh's peace and blessing upon him."

According to the *Jawāhir al-Ma'ānī*, the Prophet informed our master and Shaykh (al-Tijānī) that he, Allāh's blessing and peace on him, was the sole intermediary between him and Allāh the Exalted. He also told him that he, Allāh's blessing and peace on him, was definitely his spiritual sustainer, and the sole guardian in charge of his spiritual training in place of all the masters of the Sufi path. He informed him that not one of the spiritual masters had any favor to grant him, for everything he would receive from Allāh would come by the assistance and mediation of the Prophet. Then he advised him, "Adhere to this spiritual path (*ṭarīqa*) without seclusion (*khalwa*) or separation from people, until you arrive to spiritual station (*maqām*) promised you, while maintaining your (current) condition, without deprivation, constriction or a great deal of strenuous exertion."

The gnostic sage al-Busayrī, may Allāh have mercy on him and be well pleased with him, indicated such a condition in verse:

Excellence is not achieved by means
Of excessive abstinence nor asceticism
If it is said, "That is the medicine," say
"The kohl of the healthy (for beautification) is not
like the kohl used for eye-maladies."
The one granted the right of disposal walks where he
wills
Others walk like stones, shackled.

Sidi al-'Arabi b. Sā'iḥ said in *al-Jawāb al-Shāfī*:

"Whomever good fortune drives into entering this Aḥmadī spiritual Path – whomever Divine Providence attracts to this chain of Muḥammadan transmission, whomever Allāh's gracious favor has prepared to taste this great distinction, whomever His generosity has admitted to this marvelous store of treasure – his only remaining option is to bind himself to this greatest teacher (Shaykh Tijānī). He must finish himself at his door and cling to his threshold; and this by the path of love, submission and acceptance of his will and judgment. He must apply himself with diligence and perseverance to this noble Muḥammadan litany, observing its conditions and keeping within its precise limits. Then Allāh the Exalted may grant him success.

"And this can be achieved while he remains in his normal condition, without secluded retreat, strenuous exertion or conventional spiritual exercises of other kinds. Success will either come upon him suddenly or take him by surprise. Allāh the Exalted will favor him by removing the veil from his heart, and he will become united with the spirituality of the Shaykh, may Allāh be pleased with him, or the spirituality of the Prophet, Allāh's blessing and peace on him. Like this, his spiritual training comes by the flooding abundance (*istifāḍa*) from one of them, or from both of them together. '*That is the grace of Allāh, which He gives to whom He wills; and Allāh is the owner of infinite grace*' (Qur'ān, 57:21)."

This is the meaning of what is found in the *Jawāhir al-Maʿānī* in regards to visualizing the presence of the Shaykh or the Prophet while performing the litanies for him who is able. The *Mīzāb al-Raḥmat al-Rabbāniyya*, one of central books of the Tijāniyya, provides a lengthy explanation of this. The author said that Allāh appoints for the aspirant a brother in the spiritual path, who will take on himself the burdens of his spiritual training. Allāh the Exalted will show the aspirant the secret of his specialness, and remove from between them the veil of the guide's human nature. He will travel with his guide toward Allāh the Exalted, secretly and openly.

Whoever attains spiritual illumination (*fataḥa*) in this manner, his light will be complete, for the illumination is commensurate with the one followed. This is why Shaykh Zarrūq said, "Each individual's illumination and light is commensurate with the illumination and light of the one he follows." If someone receives directly from the texts of the Qur'ān and the Sunnah, his illumination and light will be complete, provided that he is one of those qualified to receive from them. In doing so, however, he is failing to take advantage of the light and illumination of exemplary guidance. So the Imams were wary of this approach, to the point where Ibn Madīnī,[37] may Allāh have mercy on him, said, "Ibn Mahdī[38] used to go by the word of Mālik, while Mālik used to go by the word of Sulaymān b. Yasār,[39] and Sulaymān used to go by the word of 'Umar b. al-Khaṭṭāb. The doctrine of Mālik is therefore the doctrine of 'Umar, may Allāh be pleased with him."

Junayd, may Allāh have mercy on him, said, "Whoever did not hear the traditions by sitting with scholars of understanding and by receiving proper manners from the morally refined, he will have a corrupting influence on those who follow him." Allāh the Exalted said, "*Say, 'This is my way. On clear evidence, I call to Allāh, I and all my followers. Glory be to Allāh! And I am not among the idolaters*" (Qur'ān, 12:108). And the Glorious One said: "*And this path of Mine is straight, so follow it. Follow not other ways, less you be parted from His way. This has He ordained for you, that you may fear Him*" (6:153). So understand this well.

There is no harm at this juncture in presenting some of our poems on this subject, for they contain useful advice for the truthful person. Some of the following poetic verses concern the spiritual traveler (*sālik*), while some concern the enraptured one (*majdhūb*).

Leave behind your dwellings and the beautiful
women
Leave the laden tables and soft couches
And keep company with any master successful in
combining

37 'Alī b. al-Madīnī (d. 848, Iraq) was a prominent Ḥadīth scholar who authored a work on the companions of the Prophet, *Kitāb al-Ma'rifat al-Ṣaḥāba*.

38 'Abd al-Raḥmān b. Mahdī was one of the students of the Imam Malik and his school of jurisprudence.

39 Sulayman b. Yasār (d. 733) was known as one of the seven scholars of Medina for his role in transmitting Islamic knowledge in the first century after the passing of the Prophet, peace be upon him.

The Sacred Law (sharī'a) and the Divine Reality (ḥaqīqa)
A brother, pious and ascetic, uninterested
In anything beyond what is right and proper
Beware of vain desires, and beware
The brother wrapped up in the passing of time
(To the pious brother) grant him sovereign leadership, since you know
There is none above him in this affair
Certainly he has obliterated external appearance
And has been made to arrive in the Presence of Holiness
Brought close, sanctified, and summoned
By Divine permission, with the speech of everything near (to Allāh)
When you see such a person, congratulations to you on the occasion of arrival
For seeing him is a most glorious treasure to the eyes
So the blessing of Allāh, together with peace
Upon the chosen one, from the first to the last

We also wrote:[40]

Illumination comes in the presence of the spiritual elite (al-aʿyān)
And your abandoning everything beside Him with utter conviction.

To us belong these verses as well:

The arrived ones should not assume leadership
Before permission is granted, for the secret is concealed

40 These two verses are not in the published version of the *Kāshif*, but were handwritten in the margins by Cheikh Tidiane.

I am pleased with the long silence
For it is an indication of gnosis, and of an informed state
There is no good in (mystical) interpretation at every gathering
For secrets are removed with public mention
May Allāh, Lord of the Throne, care for us, by the secret of His secret
Upon him the blessing of Allāh, for he is the disposer.

He who desires something more on this subject should keep company with the men of spiritual distinction, and serve the people of spiritual perfection.

This is how Shaykh Ibrāhīm brought forth the explanation on the subject of spiritual training. May Allāh be pleased with him and us on account of him.

Breaths of Lights in the Statements of Allāh's Exalted Folk

The light of the sun of the Divine Essence (*dhāt*) becomes manifest in the mirror of the seeker's heart, the one thirsting for the Real. This light outstrips the lights of the stars, the moon, and the sun: they are all flung into the pitch-black abyss of nonexistence. This is because the seeker has erased all other existence and lights, as in the words of the Most High, "*When the sun is folded up, and when the stars fall, losing their luster*" (81:1-2). Indeed, the seeker's rising for judgment (*qiyāma*) is a momentous occurrence (*wāqiᶜa*), not a stopping place. It is a semblance of the greater (Day of) Judgment (*al-qiyāma al-kubrā*). When the Hour's clear signs become evident, the imaginary and metaphorical lights of existence belonging to the creations are annihilated, melting away in the blazing light of Allāh's infinite Essential Being (*dhāt-Allāh al-muṭlaqa*). With the manifestation of the Absolute Exalted Truth, the (Day of) Rising is established. All existence other than His Holy Existence passes away. And what is postponed for others becomes the immediate reality for the seeker of Allāh.

Ibn ᶜAjība said in the *Īqāẓ*: "The sign of the perfection of the gnostic is his comportment (*ādāb*) in seeking, in expansion and contraction, and denial and gifting. Among everything that the Real, glorious is He, gives to His servants, He gives nothing better than the acceptance of their righteous deeds."

When the sun appears in the daytime, you do not see the stars. Similarly, when the sun of gnosis shines forth, extinguished are the traditions (*āthār*) and ceremonies (*rusūm*). Nothing remains except the Ever-Living, Self-Subsisting. It has been said:

When the morning becomes plain, its light registers
With the fading light of the stars.

It has also been said:

Between the myself and the Real, there remains no
explanation
No evidence, no signs of proof
This manifestation of the suns of the Real is a
consuming flame
I came to glow in the brilliant shining of the
Sovereign
No one knows the Real except who is known by Him
No one knows the antiquity of the conversation in
annihilation
One is not informed of the Originator (simply) by
His workmanship
You saw what happened with the Prophet in his time
This is an expression from those of singularity
Endowed with gnosis, secretly and openly.

Shaykh Aḥmad al-Tijānī on Divine Witnessing

The Hidden Pole (*al-quṭb al-maktūm*) explained the meaning of the report (of Allāh's words to the Prophet), "My servant does not cease approaching me with supererogatory worship until I love him, and when I love him, I become his hearing by which he hears" till the end of the ḥadīth. The following citation is from the *Jawāhir al-maʿānī.*

> The meaning of "until I love him" is as follows. Allāh's love for a servant entails the flood of love upon him from Allāh's Holy Essential Being. This is the most exalted of favors, and this is where the journey for all travelers ends. Whoever arrives here has all of his worldly and otherworldly needs completed. When He said, "when I love him," He is saying, "I overwhelm him in love of My Essential Being," to the extent of Allāh's words, "*He loves them, and they love Him*" (Qur'an, 5:54). Were it not for His love, glorious and exalted is He, for them, they would not have arrived at the love of His Essential Being.
>
> As for His words, "and when I love him, I become his hearing," till the end of the narration, the meaning is as follows. The servant sees in himself a divine power as if he were the Divine Sacred Essential Being, with all of its attributes and names; as if he were He, but he is not He. However, Allah the Glorious and Exalted has poured on him of the light of His attributes and names in order to

raise his station. So he comes to carry what the entirety of the creation cannot carry because of its weight. This is why some of the gnostics have said, "The one for whom is unveiled a grainsworth of divine unity (*tawḥīd*) carries the heavens and the two earths in his eyelashes," because he has been raised to this station by Divine Power. He sees by Allāh, as if his bodily presence was the Essential Being of Allāh the Exalted. He hears by Allāh.

The indication of seeing and hearing by Allāh is that in one glance, he sees all of existence, from the Divine throne to earthly canopy, with not a single grain hidden from him. He fulfills what is due to each existence, from behind and in front, to the right and left, above and below. He sees all of this in one instant, and he sees existence as a unique jewel of extraordinary apportioning, and (he sees) free of mirrors that would change its states, composition, movement, or color. All of this he sees in one glance, in one instant, in every direction, without mistaking a single grain. The reason for this vision is that eye of the spirit (*rūḥ*) has been opened. If the eye of the spirit should be opened in his bodily presence, all the creations and worlds appear before him, and not one vision is confounded. So this is the meaning of seeing by Allāh the Exalted.

Hearing by Allāh the Exalted is when a person hears all the enunciations of existence in all of the worlds, with all of their different glorifications and remembrances (of Allāh) in one instant, without obfuscation despite the plethora of enunciations and glorifications. It is as if, for each enunciation, he hears nothing other than it. Audition normally cannot distinguish one voice if there should be many voices all at once. But the comportment (*salk*) demanded of this state is to hear all of the articulations and glorifications of the existent beings without confusion.

Shaykh al-Islam Ibrāhīm Niasse on Divine Manifestation in Created Forms (tajallī ṣūrī)[41]

(Shaykh Ibrāhīm said) Divine manifestation in created forms is of three degrees. The lowest of them is what is presented to the aspirant honored with arrival (*wuṣūl*). He witnesses the figurative (created) existence as the eye of the actual existence. He sees the Divine manifestation in the mirror (of creation), but he sees neither the mirror nor Him who manifests therein. The intermediary degree is what the gnostics witness when coming to sobriety and persistence (*baqā'*). They see the Real in an impossible form. Ibn Fāriḍ said:

Beware of denying all form
Among frailties and impossible conditions

The highest degree is what the Messenger of Allāh, peace and blessing of Allāh on him, witnessed during the Night Journey (and Ascension) when he saw Allāh in the form of intimation (*ṣūrat amr*).

41 The following passage was a letter written in response to a disciple's question on the subject, and is found in Shaykh Ibrāhīm Niasse, *Jawāhir al-rasā'il*, I, 115-117.

The Divine Essential Being (*dhāt*) is infinite existence (*al-wujūd al-muṭlaq*) that elevates the aspirant above the Divine manifestation in forms. The aspirant arrives to essential interiorities where there is nothing seen and nothing manifest. So he arrives to Allāh, "*The Real has come, and falsehood has perished, for falsehood is bound to perish*" (Qur'ān, 17:81).

The essence of the Essence (*dhāt al-dhāt*) is the presence of the greatest veil, or the flood (*al-fayḍ*), the greatest spirit (*al-rūḥ al-akbar*). To this presence belongs the secret of the Divine Essential Being, a second existence, the existence of existence, the support of existence, the light of existence, the Muḥammadan reality (*al-ḥaqīqa al-Muḥammadiyya*).

The presence of Divine Uniqueness (*al-Aḥadiyya*) is the manifestation of the Divine Essential Being to Itself by Itself. There is no description of this except "*He is Allāh the Unique*" (Qur'an, 112:1). The presence of singularity (*al-wāḥidiyya*) is the manifestation of the Divine Essential Being to the Muḥammadan reality. Knowing the secret of appearance and hiddenness is when the servant knows that appearance is hiddenness, and hiddenness is appearance. This is because you know that appearance is manifestation, so understand well.

Pre-eternity is an expression of what has not ceased to be, and post-eternity is an expression of what will never be changed. In reality, both are the same, and refer to the persistence of the secret of the cosmological presences (*sir al-ḥaḍarāt*). As for the world of the unseen, this is part of witnessing, and perhaps both could be explained by my previous explanation of the world of the creation and that of the command. The being is the place of Divine manifestation. The one entrusted with worshipping Allāh in the figurative world (*al-ʿālam al-majāzī*) is the one who actualizes the real existence, the servant.

The Lord is Truth, and the servant is Truth
I wish I knew one so entrusted (mukallif)
If you say, "servant," the servant is dead
If you say say, "Lord," I am the one entrusted.

But the truth is obviously that the Lord is not like the servant, and the servant is unable to be the Lord. What is correct is that to be a servant is to be among the creation. Divine longing (*shawq*) is a state of love and ecstasy. It is like an obliteration that strikes the heart of the servant from presence of Divine compulsion. He removes himself from all personal choice, sometimes in honorable proximity with the Real, sometimes in honorable proximity with our master the Messenger of Allāh, the peace and blessing of Allāh on him, and sometimes with the Shaykh (al-Tijānī).

The (Divine) quiddity (*al-māhiya*) is primordial being: the undifferentiated Essence (*al-dhāt al-sādhij*), a sea of blindness and effacement where there is no identity. As for the Divine Identity (*huwiya*), it is the presence of "He" (*huwa*). The Name "He" with the gnostics is among the Names of the Allāh's Essential Being. Its presence is understood by the words of Allāh, "*That is because Allāh, He is the Real*" (31:30).

Divine intoxication (*sukr*)[42] is the enraptured one's freeing himself in the state of his absence from the creation and presence with the Real. Love is the attachment of the heart to the Exalted Essential Being of Allāh, enamored with Him for His sake, not for any other purpose. This is not the case except for the perfected gnostics. May Allāh make us among them by His blessing.

42 The printed version of the *Jawāhir al-rasā'il* has the word *sirr* ("secret") instead of *sukr*, apparently a mistake corrected in Cheikh Tidiane's written speech here.

Conclusion

Let us conclude this discourse of Divine longing, a discourse that does not desire an ending, with mention of the words of the Seal of Saints, Shaykh Aḥmad al-Tijānī, may Allāh be pleased with him. You will not find the following words in any book.

> I was pushed forward by a burst (*dufʿa*) from the divine presence. My beginning became my end, my end my beginning. My entirety became my every particle, and my every particle became my entirety. I became Him, and He me, but as becoming of Him, and not as becoming of me. At that moment, if I were asked a million separate questions, I would have given only one answer. Then I became like the niche of light (*miṣbāḥ*).

Shaykh al-Islām Ibrāhīm Niasse was attached to this statement, saying, "These words are the reason for my being pleased to have him as our Shaykh."

There is no doubt that these last words (of testimony to Shaykh al-Tijānī) would not emerge except from a most distinguished guidepost, the eye of sainthood (*ʿayn al-walāya*), may Allāh be pleased with him. It is no small wonder, for the speaker was the most famous scholar, the most luminous saintly pole, the most glittering star, the unique of his era, the singular of his age, the profound erudite, our master the Shaykh of Islam, al-Ḥājj Ibrāhīm b. al-Ḥājj ᶜAbd-Allāh al-Tijānī, may Allāh be pleased with him. And I should like to mention here a spiritual witnessing (*mashhad*) among many belonging to this pole of saintly aspirations. And with this, I will end this speech, so that our conclusion will be like fragrant musk. He said, may Allāh be pleased with him:

> A momentous occurrence happened to the humble servant writing this in the year 1350 after the Hijra of Muḥammad, upon him blessing and peace. It was this: I came to abide (*makathtu*) for a hundred thousand years among the days of the Lord. There I heard the purest, pre-eternal speech in intimate conversation. I became bewildered and restless, as both rapture and aching were joined in me.
>
> Then I plunged headlong into the Divine Presence, and I witnessed there the reality of the reality of the reality of the reality, in utter essentiality, exclusivity, and blind effacement. Nothing was left of sensory feelings. I dwelled like this for two hundred thousand years.
>
> Then something was with me. The existence emerged from me like shadows or smoke. And I sought after this existence, and then I was with the Messenger, from the Divine Essential Being (*dhāt*), the servant of the Divine Essential Being and Its secret. And he came close to me and stayed suspended until I disappeared in him. He became my essence. Then I was overcome with joy, for I was the beloved of the Divine Essential Being, Its secret, Its servant, Its desire. I was that which held Its comprehensive station (*martabatahā al-jāmiᶜa*), to whom the perfection of the Divine Essential Being was manifest. I resided in my state of rapture for one million years.
>
> In this manifestation in the unseen (*ghayb*), I did not find any servant of the Divine Essential Being except myself. But then there was another manifestation, unseen out of the unseen, and I saw a majestic awe (*jalāl*) in the ultimate beauty (*jamāl*). In this presence of the unseen of

> the unseen, I was called forth and named, "O Aḥmad al-Tijānī!" I knew for certain that the Real had no desire for anything, after the secret, except for me. I kept company with this servant of the Divine Essential Being, and I helped him and aided him for two million years.
>
> Then Allāh made me the father of humanity (*abū l-bashar*), and the spiritual support (*madad*) for the entirety of existent beings, the Adam of souls and spirits. I carried the trust (*amāna*), and I was called to, "*O Dāwūd, surely We have made you the khalīfa on the earth*" (Qur'ān, 38:26). I looked at the earth, and saw its state, the worlds of sense and of meaning, and then the celestial gathering, and the lower gathering. "*We built the heaven with might, and We it is who made the vast expanse. And We have laid out the earth. Gracious is He who spread it out! And all things We have created in pairs, that haply you may reflect. Therefore flee to Allāh. I am a warner to you from Him. Set up no other gods besides Allāh. I am a warner to you from Him*" (Qur'ān, 51:47-51). So I came back to my sensory feeling, and it was if the time period of the occurrence was between the even and the odd. Glory to Allāh the Majestic. He selects whom He wills for what He wills, and no one outstrips His wisdom. "*And He is not asked about what He does, but they are the ones asked*" (Qur'ān, 21:23).

With this I conclude. I ask Allāh the Blessed and Exalted to make us among those who know Him and understand Him, to make us among the elite of the elite, those passing away in Him if He should cause them to pass away, those persisting in Him if He should cause them to remain. May He guard us from being absent from Him, and not allow our souls (*nufūs*) to be fatigued in being present with Him. We ask Him by the presences of prophecy, sainthood, and their *khalīfa*, that He provide us with gnosis, by His spacious, lordly capacity, that He take us by the hands and attach our hearts to Him, Blessed and Exalted is He.[43]

---

43 These last few lines, some of them written in the margins,

O Allāh, bless our master Muḥammad, the opener of what was closed, the seal of what was past, the helper of truth by the truth, the guide to Your straight path, and on his family, commensurate with his worth and the greatness of his dimensions.

are sometimes unclear, so the translation here replicates the gathered meaning. We have also omitted the customary concluding thanking of various individuals that put the event together.

www.ingramcontent.com/pod-product-compliance
Lightning Source LLC
Chambersburg PA
CBHW070611300426
44113CB00010B/1491
9780991381333

ما قاله العارفون بالله
عن المعرفة بالله

الإمام الشيخ التجاني علي سيس
إمام المسجد الجامع بمدينة كولخ المحروسة
جمهورية السنغال

مقدمة بقلم الإمام فخرالدين الأويسي المدني

الحمد لله و العبد لله و الصلاة و السلام على وسيلتنا رسول الله و آله و صحبه و من والاه،

و بعد فإن مما لا شك و لا ريب فيه عند أرباب العقول هو أن الخالق جل و علا خلقنا لأجل معرفته و تعارفا لذاته. يقول الله تعالى في كتابه المجيد: "و ما خلقت الجن و الإنس إلا ليعبدون". و قد فسره ترجمان القرآن ابن عباس ب"يعرفون".

إذن فالمعرفة بالله هي غاية الوجود و السبب في كل موجود. و لذا وجب على كل عاقل و لبيب أن يتحرى معرفة خالقه و الأسباب الموصلة لذلك. لأن "من لم ينل معرفة الرحمن فقد ضاع عمره مع الازمان".

و عليه فيسعدنا أن نقدم لرواد المعرفة و طلاب الحقيقة هذه الرسالة الجليلة الصغيرة الحجم و العظيمة المعنى لأحد كبار العارفين و المعرفين بالله في عصرنا، ألا و هو الشيخ الإمام التجاني على سيس حفظه الله و رعاه و امدنا بنوره و سره.

فالشيخ التجاني سيس (بكسر السينين) لا يكتب عن المعرفة من ناحية نظرية فقط . كلا! بل يكتب كعامل و ناشط في مجال المعارف الإلهية، يربي و يسلك المريدين على المعرفة على الدوام، و لا يحصى عدد من فتح الله عليهم بالمعرفة العيانية الشهودية على يده الكريمة و تحت نظرته الشريفة.

و لم لا و هو سليل و خريج دار المعرفة الكبرى و معقل التربية و السلوك و الجذب في قرننا الاخير! نعم جده امام العارفين و شيخ المربين الغوث الأعظم صاحب الفيضة التجانية و خليفة الحضرة الربانية مولانا الشيخ إبراهيم نياس رضي الله عنه، الذي تفجرت على يديه بحار المعرفة بالله فعمت المشرق و المغرب. "و ليس يصح في الأذهان شيء - إذا احتاج النهار الى دليل". و الشيخ الجد

هو الذي سمى مؤلفنا باسم ممد العارفين و قطب الأقطاب المحمديين مولانا الشيخ أحمد التجاني قدس الله سره و امدنا بممده، تيمنا و تبركا و ترجيا و استبشارا.

و أبوه خليفة الشيخ صاحب الفيضة و باب علومه و و صهره و مربي أولاده و خلفاءه، العارف الأكبر و البدر المنير الأنور سيدي علي سيس رضي الله عنه. و أمه المصونة كبرى بنات الشيخ صاحب الفيضة و أول من تربي و فتح عليهم من أولاده السيدة فاطمة الزهراء نياس حفظها الله و رعاها. و أخوه الذي خلفه في إمامة الجامع الإبراهيمي الأعظم بكولخ (سنغال) شيخنا و سندنا و مربينا القطب الإمام الحسن سيس قدس الله سره و جزاه عنا و عن سائر الأحباب خير الجزاء.

فجدير بمن يطلب معرفة خالقه و مولاه أن يقرأ ما كتبه مثل الشيخ التجاني سيس بكامل الامعان و الإذعان لأن الشيء من معدنه لا يستغرب! و لولا المربي لما عرفت ربي!

فلا سبيل الى معرفة الرب اليوم إلا بواسطة دين الإسلام و المشرب المحمدي و امام أهل المعرفة في الإسلام هو خاتم الولاية المحمدية سيدنا أحمد التجاني رضي ألله عنه و باب فيضه و مدده الأعظم هو مولانا صاحب الفيضة التجانية رضي الله عنه.

و شيخنا الإمام التجاني سيس يتكلم نيابة عن هذه الحضرات الثلاث و هو خير ممثل لها اليوم. فهنيئا لمن تعلق بهذه الحضرات الشريفة و انخرط في سلكها و سلوكها و سقي من هذه المناهل العذبة. فمن ذاق عرف، و من عرف غرف!

و نترككم و هذه الرسالة الشريفة مع قولة أحد أساطين الفيضة سيدي الشيخان:

بحر المياه يكفي منه الشراب و
بحر المعارف لا يكفيه سوى الغرق

و نختم بدعاء الشيخ رضي الله عنه:

و اكشف لبرهام الحجاب
و نجه من العقاب

و ما له من الصحاب
بجاه عبدك العلي

اللّٰهُمَّ افتح علينا فتوح العارفين و أحشرنا في حزب سيد الأولين و الآخرين صلى الله عليه و على اله و صحبه أجمعين.

و كتبه،
تلميذ المؤلف، العبد الفقير فخرالدين الأويسي
عفا الله عنه

بِسْمِ اللَّهِ الرَّحْمَنِ الرَّحِيمِ

الحمد لله الذي آخى بين الأرواح، وألف بينها قبل ظهور الأشباح، وعلمنا على لسان نبيه أن الأرواح جنود مجندة، ما تعارف منها إئتلف، وما تناكر منها اختلف. يقول الله تبارك وتعالى: ﴿وإذ أخذ الله من بنى آدم من ظهورهم ذريتهم ألست بربكم قالوا: بلى﴾

فأجابوا بالباء التي بها كان ما كان، وبها يكون ما يكون إلى يوم اللقاء. وصلى الله وسلم على سر الذات، ونور الذات، سيدنا محمد نور الوجود، ومدد الوجود، من لا وجود إلا وجوده، ولا نور إلا نوره، ولا مدد إلا مدده، صلاة تعرفنا بها إياه. يقول رب العزة: "كنت كنزا لم أعرف، فأحببت أن أعرف، فخلقت خلقا، فتعرفت إليهم، فبي عرفوني". وكلمة

” فبي“ عددها بالجملة 92، وهوعدد حروف اسم ”محمد“، أي؛ فبمحمد عُرِف تبارك وتعالى. وعلى آله الأطهار، وصحابته الأخيار، والتابعين وتابعيهم بإحسان إلى يوم الدين.

أما بعد؛
حضرات السادة الوزراء والأمراء والمدراء، أصحاب السعادة، حضرات الأئمة والمشايخ والمقدمين، حضرة السيد الشريف المنيف، العلامة الشريف عمر بن عبدالعزيز، الذي يترأس هذه الجلسة المباركة الميمونة، مع إخوته الشرفاء الأكارم، أيهاالاخوة والأخـوات الوافدين من شتى بقاع الأرض لحضور المولد؛ السلام عليكم ورحمة الله تعالى و بركاته!

يسرني أن ألتقي بهذا الجمع الغفير من الأحباب من أهل ساحل العاج في هذا المكان المبارك، وممن وفدوا من دول الجوار، للمذاكرة فيما بيننا في موضوع ”المعرفة بالله“. والطريقة - كما قيل - إنما هي ذكر ومذاكرة. فنرجو من الله تعالى أن يفيدنا بمايسمعنا، ويسمعنا ما يفيدنا، في سيرنا

اللامنتهي إليه، إنه مجيب من رفع الشكوى إليه، فبه أقول - وما قولي إلا به منه وإليه.

حقيقة المعرفة بالله

المعرفة هى: العلم؛ فكل علم معرفة؛ وكل معرفة علم؛ وكل عالم بالله عارف؛ وكل عارف عالم. وأما في اصطلاح القوم فالمعرفة صفة من عرف الحق سبحانه بأسمائه وصفاته؛ ثم صدق الله تعالى في معاملاته، ثم تنقى عن أخلاقه الرديئة وأفاته؛ ثم طال بالباب وقوفه ودام بالقلب عتكافه فحظي من الله تعالى بجميل إقباله وصدق الله في جميع أقواله؛ وانقطع عنه هواجس نفسه؛ ولم يضع بقلبه أي خاطر يدعوه إلى غيره؛ فإذا صار من الخَلِق أجنبيًا ومن آفات نفسه بريًا، و من المساكنات و الملاحظات نقيًا، و دام في السر مع الله تعالى مناجاته، وكان في كل لحظة إليه رجوعه وصار محدثا من قبل الحق سبحانه بتعريف أسراره فيما يجريه من تصاريف أقداره، يسمى عند ذلك عارفا وتسمى حالته معرفة. **وبالجملة فبمقدار أجنبيته**

عن نفسه تحصل معرفته بربه.

قال نبي الله داود عليه السلام :"يـارب كيف الوصول اليـك؟". قال الرب جل جلاله: «اترك نفسك و تعال».

قاله الإمام أبي القاسم عبد الكريم بن هوازن القشيري المتوفي سنة 465 ه رضي الله عنه وأرضاه ورحمه برحمته الواسعة.

وسئل القطب المكتوم سيدنا أحمد التجاني رضي الله عنه عن حقيقة المعرفة بالله تعالى فأجاب بقوله: المعرفة الحقيقية أخذ الله للعبد أخذا لا يعرف له أصلا ولا فصلا ولا سببا ولا يتعقل فيه كيفية مخصوصة ولا يبقى له شعور بحسه وشواهده وممحواته ومشيئته وإرادته بل تقع عن تجل إلهي ليس له بداية ولا نهاية ولا يوقف له على حد ولا نهاية.

قال أيضا في جواهر المعاني : أهل العرفان هم الغائبون في الله عن كل فان مشاهدون لجلال الله وجماله العالمون بصفاته وأسمائه.

وقال قطب العارفين صاحب الفيضة التجانية، مولانا الشيخ ابراهيم إنياس: المعرفة هي رسوخ الروح وتمكينه في حضرة المشاهدة مع الفناء التام والبقاء بالله. فالعارف عند الصوفية من يرى الغير العين، أي شهود الحق في الغير. والعارف عندي؛ من فني في الذات مرة وفني في الصفة مرتين أو ثلاثا وفني في الاسم مرة، وأثبت الوجود بالحقائق الثلاث، وأثبت الاسماء بالاسم. وهذا مقام دونه القتاد، وتفتت الأكباد، ولا ينال ببذل الأموال والأولاد، وصاحب هذا المقام كامل اليقظة بالله وبحكمه وأحكامه راضيا بمجاري الأقدار كمال الرضا، مرضيا فيستحق قوله:

«فادخلى فى عبادى وادخلى جنتى».

وقال أيضا - رضي الله عنه - بأنها : الكشف عن أسماء الله وصفاته ونتيجتها مراقبة الله و إخلاص العمل له.

و قال أيضا : حقيقة المعرفة؛ شهود الكمال الذاتي :»ليس كمثله الشئ«.

وقال أيضا : من عرف الله فليس له مع الخلق لذة ومن عرف الدنيا فليس له في معيشته لذة ومن انفتحت عين بصيرته بهت و لم يتفرغ للكلام.

و قال الشيخ الأكبر محيي الدين ابن عربي : اعلم أن المعرفة ضربان : معرفة العام، و معرفة الخاص! أما الأولى فهي معرفة تحصل بالاستدلال و تسمى علم اليقين، أما الثانية فعلى قسمين: عين اليقين ومعرفة حق اليقين، فالقسم الأول معرفة تحصل بواسطة الشهود وهي مقام خواص الأولياء، وأما القسم الثاني فهو معرفة تحصل للروح بعين المشاهدة وذلك يكون عند سلامة حواس القلب من جميع الكدوراتا لنفسانية وتجرده عن التعلقات البدنية وصفائه عن الصفات البشرية فهناك تظهر للروح معرفة الله تعالى.

وقال الشبلي : العارف لا يكون لغيره لاحظا، ولا بكلام غيره لافظا، ولا يرى لنفسه غير الله تعالى حافظا.

وقال بعضهم : المعرفة أن يميتك الحق عن نفسك، و يحييك به.

وقيل : العارف أنس بذكر الله فأوحشه من خلقه وافتقر إلى الله فأغناه عن خلقه، وذل له تعالى فأعزه في خلقه.

وقال أبو الطيب السامري : المعرفة طلوع الحق على الأسرار بمواصلة الأنوار.

وقيل : العارف فوق ما يقول، والعالم دون ما يقول.

وقال الجنيد : العارف من نطق الحق عن سره وهو ساكت.

سئل يعقوب السوسي : هل يتأسف العارف على شيء غير الله عز وجل؟ فقال :
وهل يرى غيره فيتأسف عليه؟!
قلت : فبأي عين ينظر إلى الأشياء ؟
فقال : بعين الفناء والزوال.

وقيل : العارف تبكي عينه ويضحك قلبه.

و قال الجنيد: لا يكون العارف عارفا حتى يكون كالأرض يطؤه البر والفاجر، وكالسحاب يظل كل شيء، وكالمطر، يسقي ما يحب، ومالا يحب.

وقال أبويزيد : إنما نالوا المعرفة بتضييع ما لهم والوقوف مع ماله.

قال ابن عطاء الله : المعرفة على ثلاثة أركان : الهيبة، والحياء، والأنس.

وقيل لذي النون المصري :بم عرفت ربك ؟ قال : عرفت ربي بربي، ولولا ربي لماعرفت ربي.

وقيل : العالم يقتدي به، والعارف يهتدي به.

سئل بعض المشايخ: بم عرفت الله تعالى؟ فقال: بلمعة لمعت بلسان مأخوذ عن التمييز المعهود، ولفظة جرت على لسان هالك مفقود يشير إلى وجد ظاهر ويخبر عن سر سائر هو بما اظهره، وغيره بما اشكله ثم أنشد:

نطقت بلا نطق هو النطق إنه
لك النطق لفظا أو يبين عن النطق
تراءيت كى أخفى وقد كنت خافيا
وألمعت لي برقا فانطقت بالبرق

وقيل عن صفة العارف: الذي لا يكدره شيء،

ويصفوبه كل شيء.

وقال ذو النون: علامة العارف ثلاثة: لا يطفىء نور معرفته نور ورعه، ولا يعتقد باطنا من العلم ينقض عليه ظاهرا من الحكم، ولا تحمله كثرة نعم الله عز وجل، عليه على هتك أستار محارم الله.
وقال أبو سعيد الخراز: المعرفة تأتي من عين الجود وبذل المجهود.

سئل الجنيد عن قول ذى النون المصري في صفة العارف: «كان هاهنا فذهب». فقال الجنيد: العارف لا يحصره حال عن حال، ولا يحجبه منزل من التنقل في المنازل، فهو مع أهل كل مكان يمثل الذي هو فيه يجد مثل الذى يجدون، وينطق فيها بمعالمها لينتفعوا بها.

قال محمد بن الفضل: المعرفة حياة القلب مع الله تعالى.

سئل ابن السماك: متى يعرف العبد أنه على حقيقة المعرفة؟ قال: اذا شاهد الحق بعين اعتباره فانيا عن كل ما سواه.

قال يحي بن معاذ رحمه الله : المعرفة قرب القلب الى القريب، ومراقبة الروح للحبيب، والانفراد عن الكل بالملك المجيب.

يروى أن الله تعالى أوحى الى داود عليه السلام : يا دواد اعرفني واعرف نفسك فتفكر داود فقال: إلهي عرفتك بالفردانية، والقدرة، والبقاء وعرفت نفسي بالعجز و الفناء.

قلت: ومعرفة الله سبحانه وتعالى بهذا المعنى هو أقصى غاية الناسكين، ومنتهى آمال السادة المتقين، وقد دفع القوم في سبيل ذلك الغالي والنفيس، وأفنوا فيه الأعمار، وغادروا من أجله الأقطار وتكبدوا المشقات، وعانوا الويلات، حتى يظفروا به، ومع ذلك فقد رجع بعضهم خاوي الوفاض دون أن يحقق شيئا من ذلك، لإخلاله ببعض الشروط، أو إخفاقه في الصبر على بعض الأمور.

ويكفيك مثالا على ذلك قصة موسى مع صاحبه الخضر عليهما وعلى نبينا الصلاة والسلام، حيث لم يستطع موسى عليه السلام، ذلك النبي العظيم

- الذي يعد من أولي العزم - لم يستطع الصبر على امتحان الخضر، فرجع منه دون أن يحظى بشيء من ذلك العلم اللدني الذى ذهب من أجله.

هذا وقد كان يعتبر هذا العلم من الكنوز النادرة، وصاحبه هو الكبريت الأحمر، إلا أنه بعد ظهور الختم التجاني فقد طوى المسافات، وقرب المساحات، فانتشر العلم بين أصحابه، وفشا بين أتباعه. ولما ظهر صاحب الفيضة التجانية مولانا شيخ الاسلام الشيخ إبراهيم بن الحاج عبد الله انياس، فاضت العلوم والمعارف، فشرب منها كل متعرض وغارف، حتى أصبحت المعرفة بالله تعم كافة الأقطار، ويتنعم بها كل المنتسبين إلى هذا القطب الهمام، وما أكثرهم في هذا الزمان، وهم الأئمة والعلماء, والسادة والأمراء، وهم في كل بلاد نجوما يقتدى بهم، ونباريس يهتدى بهم، وهم المتفوقون في كافة الفنون والناجحين في جميع الشئون، فأكرم بهم وبشيخهم، رضي الله عنه وعنا به ونفعنا به آمين.

الطريق إلى المعرفة

قال صاحب الفيضة التجانية مولانا الشيخ ابراهيم نياس نقلا عن الإمام العلامة العارف بالله سيدى محمد اليدالي فى شرح خاتمة التصوف مانصه:

وقال بعضهم: أقرب الطرق إلى دخول الحضرة ذكر الله، لأن الاسم لايفارق مسماه، فلا يزال الذاكر يذكر والحجب تتمزق شيئا فشيئا، حتى يقع الشهود القلبي لله، وحينئذ يستغنى عن الذكر بمشاهدة المذكور، ومرادهم بحضرة الله حيث أطلقت انكشاف الحجب، فتدخلها وأنت قاعد مكانك. الثانية قال في شرح شهية السماع: لايقرب عبد إلى حضرته تعالى إلا أن يستحي منه حق الحياء، ولايصلح لة ذلك الا أن يحصل له الكشف ورفع الحجاب، ولا يصلح له ذلك إلا بملازمة الذكر ولايصلح له مقام الإخلاص

الكامل وهو شهود الأعمال أنها خلق الله تعالى إلا بمداومة الذكر، ولا تخمد الأمراض الباطنية إلا به، ولا تنقطع الخواطر الشيطانية إلا به، ولا تضعف الخواطر النفسانية إلا به، وبمداومته يزول الهم والغم في الدنيا فإنهما بقدر الغفلة عن الله، فلا يلومن العبد إلا نفسه إذا ترادفت عليه الهموم والغموم، فإن ذلك إنما هو جزاؤه بقدر إعراضه عن ربه، فمن أراد دوام السرور فليداوم على الذكر. وقد يقنع بعض المغرورين بمجلس الذكر صباحا ومساء مع الغفلة عن الله فيما بينهما، وذلك لا ينجع بالسالك إلى منازل القوم، وربما يحتج بحديث "اذا ذكر العبد ربه أول النهار ساعة وآخر النهار ساعة غفر له مابينهما" والمغفرة لا ترقى فيها، وغايتها أن تلحق المذنب بمن لا يذنب ذلك الذنب لا أنها تلحقه بمن فعل الطاعات، فافهم. ومراد القوم دوام الترقي مع الأنفاس فى المقامات وذلك بدوام ذكر الله، ثم إنهم لا يرون أنهم قاموا بذرة واحدة من واجب حق الله تعالى اه منه بلفظه. انتهى من كاشف الالباس.

فالمعرفة عند القوم حصول العلم بالله تعالى ذاتا وصفاتا وأسماء وأفعالا، وهي أوجب الواجبات وأسنى الكرامات لأنها أصل الإيمان وغاية الاسلام. والمعرفة بالله هى منتهى غاية الكمال الانساني ومكانة عالية المدرك غالية المثال فلا ينال مكانة المعرفة بالله إلا الذين جازوا المراحل كلها بقدم ثابت، وإيمان قوى وقلب سليم، فلا يكون العارف بالله عارفا له إلا إذا طوى المراحل فى سيره إلى الله، فمعرفة الانسان لله دونها كل معرفة، ولا يقوى أن يبلغ هذه الدرجة إلا الذى ابتدأ سيره على الأدب فاستقام بظهره وباطنه على الأدب، ونفذ الأمر والمراد فى أعماله وأقواله بغير كفة ولا منة واستكملت صفاته تتمة نور الكمال الرباني فيترقى من كامل إن أكمل، واقتبست أخلاقه من الأدب نوراً فاستضاء بالهدى وأضاء بالحق وتغذت روحه من الحقائق قوتا، فأحرم لله مخلصا له الدين، وعمر قلبه بالايمان فأخلص النية ظاهرا و باطنا، فمن عرف الله حق معرفته سار في هذا الكون وهو المثال لفضائل الصفات العالية، المؤدب فى قوله وعمله وحاله، المحب للخير لأخيه المؤمن كما يحبه لنفسه، المتوجه إلى الله طاهر القلب، مكتمل

العقيدة، ثابت الايمان، راسخ القدم، سامي الذوق، مراده الله.

وقال شيخ الاسلام مولانا الشيخ إبراهيم نياس أيضا:

أما معرفة كيفية السعى إليه فهى متابعة الرسول صلى الله عليه وسلم فى سائر قوله وفعله وحاله وخلقه بإقامة حقوق الله تعالى فى السر والعلانية، مخلصا لله تعالى من جميع الشوائب الدنيوية والأخروية، وأن يكون ذلك لله تعالى تعظيما وإجلالا لله على بساط الرضى والتسليم والتفويض والاعتماد عليه تعالى فى كل شى.

قال العلامة سيدي محمد بن المشري السباعي السائحي في كتاب "روض المحب الفاني فيما تلقيناه من سيدي أبي العباس التجاني" حكاية عن القطب المكتوم سيدي أحمد التجاني قدس سره:

وأما ما هو حقيقة الشيخ الواصل فهو الذي رفعت له جميع الحجب عن كمال النظر إلى الحضرة الإلهية نظرا عيانيا، وتحقيقا يقينيا. فإن الأمر أوله

محاضرة؛ وهو مطالعة الحقائق من وراء ستر كثيف، ثم مكاشفة، وهو مطالعة الحقائق من وراء ستر رقيق، ثم مشاهدة؛ وهو تجلي الحقائق بلا حجاب ولكن مع خصوصية، ثم معاينة؛ وهو مطالعة الحقائق بلا حجاب ولا خصوصية ولا بقاء للغير والغيرية عينا وأثرا، وهو مقام السحق والمحق والدك وفناء الفناء. فليس في هذا إلا معاينة الحق في الحق بالحق،!

فلم يبق إلا الله لا شيء غيره
فما ثم موصول وما ثم واصل

ثم حياة، وهي تمييز المراتب بمعرفة جميع خصوصياتها ومقتضياتها ولوازمها وما تستحقه من كل شيء ومن أي حضرة، كل مرتبة منها ولماذا وجدت وماذا يراد منها وما يؤول إليه أمرها، وهو مقام إحاطة العبد بعينه ومعرفته جميع أسراره وخصوصياته، ومعرفة ما هي الحضرة الإلهية وما هي عليه من العظمة والجلال والنعوت العالية والعلية والكمال، معرفة ذوقية ومعاينة يقينية.

فصاحب هذه المرتبة هو الذي تشق إليه المهامه في طلبه لكن مع هذه الصفة فيه كمال إذن الحق له سبحانه وتعالى إذنا خاصا في هداية عبيده وتوليته إرشادهم إلى الحضرة الإلهية.

توحيد العارفين

قال العلامة سيدي محمد بن المشري السباعي السائحي في كتاب «روض المحب الفاني فيما تلقيناه من سيدي أبي العباس التجاني»:

سئل رضي الله عنه (يعني الختم التجاني) عن توحيد العارفين والفرق بينه وبين توحيد المتكلمين، فأجاب رضي الله عنه: أما توحيد المتكلمين فهو دفع الشبه القادحة في صحة التوحيد من كل ما يوجب نقصا أو سلب كمال أو جهلا في وصف الباري سبحانه وتعالى. ودفع هذه كلها إنما هو بالحجج العقلية القائمة على المقدمات اليقينية. فأصحابه في تعب عظيم من كثرة توارد الشبه وما يصحبها منكثرة الوساوس والتخليط. وأما توحيد العارفين فهو عبادة إله واحد بالرضا والتسليم لحكم إله واحد ولا يعتمد في جميع أطواره إلا

على الإله الواحد، ولا يتوجه بهمته وقلبه الا إلى الإله الواحد، فيتبرأ من حوله وقوته للحول والقوة المتصف بهما إله واحد، ولا يحب إلا إلها وأحدا، ولا يشتاق في جميع مآربه إلا إلى إله واحد، ويجعل مبدأ قصده وغاية مطلبه ووسط ما يسلكه بين المبدئي والغاية هو الاله الواحد.

وفي كل هذا بمفارقة الهوى ظاهرا وباطنا وعينا وأثرا، والبعد إلى الغاية القصوى من تلبيسات النفس والهوى والشيطان، ومتى وقع فيه ولو أقل قليل من متابعة الهوى، ولو مثقال ذرة أو هبئة فما وحد إله واحدا، ولا صفت له العبودية لإله واحد، ثم إذا هم له هذا التوحيد وتشيد له حصنه واستقر فيه وغرق في بحر الرضا والتسليم علما منه بأن الإله الواحد لا يصح الخروج عن حكمه، حلوه ومره، خيره وشره، ولا اختيار لأحد معه، فإن كان اختار معه كان إلها معه.

فمن صح له ما تقدم من الأوصاف المذكورة استراح من معاناة المقادير، وجلس على بساط النعيم والتنعم، لخلعه لحلل التعب مما كان فيه من

نكد التدبير، فهناك جلس مع الله على بساط القرب والمؤانسة، فلا تسأل عما يجده من المنح والمواهب، وبلوغ الآمال ووجوه الرغائب، من العز والمجد الأقصى والمكارم التي لا تحد ولا تحصى.

فهذا هو توحيد العارفين الذي لما ذكره القطب مولاي عبد العزيز الدباغ رضي الله عنه لصاحبه العالم الكبير سيدي أحمد بن مبارك استراح من تعب ما كان فيه من دفع الشبه التي تتوارد على المتكلمين، وأما توحيد العارفين فلا تلحقه الشبه.

ثم قال رضي الله عنه:

مثالها مثال شخصين أحدهما توغلت فيه معضلة الأدواء، وكلما زال عنه شيء جاء أعظم منه، فلأجلها اعتنى بالبحث في كثرة علم الطب ومعرفة العلل وأصولها من أين نشأت ومعرفة الأدوية المزيلة لتلك العلل، وكيفية تناولها كما وكيفا ووقتا وافرادا وتركيبا. فهو في تعب عظيم من معانات هذه العلوم، ومتى أخطأ في شيء منها وقع له الضرر وقد فاته أكثر مطالبه لاشتغاله بهذا العلم

وفنونه. وأما الآخر فقد نشأ كامل الصحة والقوة، قد سلمه الله من جميع الآفات وعوارض البليات، و لم تقع عليه آفة قط ولا رآها بعينه فتغافل عن تعلم جميع علم الطب وعن جميع مقتضياته ولوازمه.

فإذا لامه الأول بهذا قال له: جهلك بالطب عليك فيه ضررعظيم. قال له الآخر: إنما يحتاج للطب أمثالك الذين توغلت فيهم العلل، وأما أنا فلا أعرف الداء فليست بي حاجة إلى الدواء.

وأما عن السوال عن لماذا لم يظهروا هذا التوحيد في الكتب والدواوين حتى يعم نفعه؟

قال الجواب: إنهم ما كتموه وأن ذلك التوحيد هو الذي بعثت به الرسل كلها وهو الذي يظهر لعامة الخلق، وإنما ترك ودرست طريقه لأعراض عامة الناس عنه لميلهم إلى شقاشق علم الكلام والبحث في قواعده وأصوله بالحجج العقلية والمقدمات اليقينية، ظنا منهم أن تلك هي الغاية في التقرب إلى الله تعالى وكمال العلم به، وجهلوا أن ذلك هو غاية البعد عن الله والضلال.

فإن السبب الذي أوقع العامة في هذا مخالطتهم لعلوم أوائل الفلاسفة فوجدوهم قرروا في علومهم علم التوحيد الحق هو البحث في العلم الإلهي بالقواعد العقلية والمقدمات المنطقية، فصرفهم الله بذلك عن معرفة الحق ومثاله وعن التقرب بما يقرب إلى الله ومعرفة جلاله. وحيث كان الصحابة لم يخالطوا هذا العلم كانوا قائمين على توحيد الرسل الذى كان جنا ثماره وذوق حلاوة يانعه من صريح الأخبار الألهية بما في كتب الله التي بعثها إلى خلقه مع رسله وما نطقت به رسله في تعليم العامة من العلم بالله ومعرفة عظمته وجلاله.

فلما دخل على الصدر الثالث علوم الفلسفة وسمعوا فيها في فن التوحيد شقاشق عربية تستحيلها نفوس أهل الفضول المعرضين عن الله تعالى. وكل من حصل منهم صال بها على العامة والجاهلين بها مدعيا أن الذي وصل إليه في رقية العلم هو غاية القصوى فى العلم بالله ومعرفة جلاله، ويصرحون على العامة أن من لا يعلمها كأنه لا يعلم شيئا من العلم. فتتبعتهم نفوس العامة لشدة ميلها إلى الفضول حيث رأوا لهم

التعظيم البالغ الغاية في قلوب العامة والملوك والأمـراء بسبب تتابع الأعصار على هذا خلفا عن سلف من غير معارض ولا زاجر، نسي علم التوحيد الذي بعث به الرسل وصار السالكون على توحيد الرسل المعرضون على توحيد الفلاسفة هم المسمون بالصوفية والعارفين. وصار السالكون على توحيد الفلاسفة هم المسمون باهل علم الكلام.

وأما من تنزل إلى فن علم الكلام من العارفين كالأشعري والسنوسي وأمثالهما رضي الله عنهم، إنما أرادوا الرفق بالعامة لما كان توحيد الرسل لا يستجيبون له إلا بالسيف. فتنزلوا لهم باقرار حجج عقلية يدركونها في نفوسهم ليستجيبوا بذلك لأمر الله باختيارهم. فرأوا أن ذلك خير من السيف لكون صاحبه لا يدخل في الدين إلا قهرا وجبرا. فهذا هو السبب الذي حملهم على التنزل إلى فن علم الكلام. وأما وحدة الوجود فسيأتي له رضي الله عنه الكلام عليها إن شاء الله تعالى.
انتهى كلام رضي الله عنه، من كتاب روض المحب الفاني.

هذا وقد قسم الامام الغزالي رحمه الله في الأحياء التوحيد أربع مراتب؛ إلى لب وإلى لب اللب، وإلى قشر وإلى قشر القشر...إلى أن قال: فالرتبة الأولى من التوحيد أن يقول الإنسان بلسانه لا إله إلا الله وقلبه غافلا عنه أو منكرا له كتوحيد المنافقين. والثانية أن يصدق بمعنى اللفظ قلبه كما صدق به عموم المسلمين وهو اعتقاد العوام. والثالثة أن يشاهد ذلك بطريق الكشف بواسطة نور الحق وهو مقام المقربين وذلك بأن يرى أشياء كثيرة ولكن يراها على كثرتها صادرة من الواحد القهار. والرابعة أن لا يرى في الوجود إلا واحدا وهى مشاهدة الصديقين و ما تسميه الصوفية الفناء في التوحيد لأنه من حيث لا يرى إلا واحدا فلا يرى نفسه أيضا وإذا لم ير نفسه لكونه مستغرقا بالتوحيد كان فانيا عن نفسه في توحيده بمعنى أنه فنى عن رؤية نفسه والخلق.

وقال محمد بن موسى الواسطي: جملة التوحيد أن كل ما ينطق به اللسان أو يشير إليه البيان من تعظيم أو تجريد أو تفريد فهو معلول والحقيقة وراء ذلك.

ويقول سيدنا وشيخنا أحمد التجاني رضي الله عنه: ما دمت ترى أنك موجود والله موجود فثم اثنان، فأين التوحيد؟ لا توحيد إلا إذا كان التوحيد بالله من الله إلى الله والعبد لا مدخل له فيه ولا مخرج، وهذا لا يصح إلا من طريق الفناء.

إذا تقرر انفراد الحق بالوجود فلا تتعد همتك إلى غيره إذ هو مفقود. وقال ابن عجيبة في شرح قوله في الحكم «لا تتعد نية همتك إلى غيره فالكريم لا تتخطاه الآمال».

إذا تعلقت همتك أيها المريد بشيء تريد تحصيله فردها إلى الله ولا تتعلق بشيء سواه لأنه سبحانه كريم على الدوام ونعمه سخاء على مر الليالي والأيام والكريم لا تتخطاه الآمال وهو يحب أن يسئل فيجيب السؤال.

ضرورة صحبة العارف

اعلم أن المريد لا ينتفع بعلوم الشيخ وأحواله إلا إذا انقاد له الانقياد التام، ووقف عند أمره ونهيه، مع اعتقاده الأفضلية والأكملية، ولا يغني أحدهما عن الآخر كحال بعض الناس يعتقد في الشيخ غاية الكمال ويظن أن ذلك يكفيه في نيل غرضه، وحصول مطلبه، وهو غير ممتثل ولا فاعل لما يأمره الشيخ به، أو ينهاه عنه. وإليك أقوال بعض العلماء العارفين بالله في ضرورة الصحبة وفوائدها.

قال ابن عجيبة في ايقاظ الهمم:

قال شيخ شيوخنا سيدي علي الجمل رضي الله عنه في كتابه: أعلم أنه لا يقرب طالب الوصول إلى الله تعالى شيء مثل جلوسه مع عارف بالله إن وجده. ثم قال: الجلوس مع العارف بالله أفضل من العزلة

والعزلة أفضل من الجلوس مع العوام الغافلين والجلوس مع العامي الغافل أفضل من الجلوس مع الفقير الجاهل، وكما إن العارف بالله يجمع بين المريد ومولاه بنظرة أو بكلمة كذلك الفقير الجاهل بالله ربما أتلف المريد عن مولاه بنظرة أو كلمة فما فوقها.

هذا وفي قصة النبي موسى عليه السلام مع الخضر دليل قوتي على ضرورة صحبة شيخ عارف، والتسليم له والانقياد لأمره من أجل الوصول إلى الغاية المرجوة والحصول على المعارف السنية.

وقال الأمير العارف بالله عبد القادر الجزائري في كتابه «المواقف» :

فهذا موسى عليه السلام، مع جلالة قدره وفخامة أمره طلب لقاء الخضر عليه السلام وسأل السبيل إلى لقيه، وتجشم مشاق ومتاعب في سفره، كما قال: ﴿لَقَدْ لَقِينَا مِن سَفَرِنَا هَـٰذَا نَصَبًا﴾ (الكهف: 62)

ومع هذا كله لما لم يمتثل نهيا واحدا، وهو قوله: ﴿فَلَا تَسْأَلْنِي عَن شَيْءٍ حَتَّىٰ أُحْدِثَ لَكَ مِنْهُ ذِكْرًا﴾ (الكهف: 70)

ما انتفع بعلوم الخضر عليه السلام، مع يقين موسى عليه السلام الحازم أن الخضر أعلم منه بشهادة الله تعالى، لقوله تعالى عندما قال موسى عليه السلام: لا أعلم أحد أعلم مني (بلى، عبدنا خضر) وما خص علما دون علم، بل عمم.

وكان موسى عليه السلام أولا ما علم ان استعداده لا يقبل شيئا من علوم الخضرعليه السلام. وأما الخضر عليه السلام، فإنه علم ذلك أول وهلة فقال: ﴿إِنَّكَ لَن تَسْتَطِيعَ مَعِيَ صَبْرًا﴾ (الكهف: 67)

وهذا من شواهد علمية الخضر عليه السلام فلينظر العاقل إلى أدب هذين السيدين.

قال موسى عليه السلام:﴿هَلْ أَتَّبِعُكَ عَلَىٰ أَن تُعَلِّمَنِ مِمَّا عُلِّمْتَ رُشْدًا﴾ (الكهف: 66)

أي: هل تأذن في اتباعك، لأتعلم منك؟ ففي هذه الكلمات من حلاوة الأدب ما يذوقها كل سليم الذوق.

وقال الخضر عليه السلام:﴿فَإِنِ اتَّبَعْتَنِي فَلَا تَسْأَلْنِي عَنْ شَيْءٍ حَتَّىٰ أُحْدِثَ لَكَ مِنْهُ ذِكْرًا﴾ (الكهف: 70)

وما قال: فلا تسألني، وسكت، فيبقى موسى عليه السلام حيران متعطشا، بل وعده أنه يحدث له ذكرا، أي: علما بالحكمة فيما فعل، أو ذكرا: بمعنى تذكرا.

يقول ابن عطاء الله السكندري رضى الله عنه:

وينبغي لمن عزم على الاسترشاد، وسلوك طريق الرشاد، أن يبحث عن شيخ من أهل التحقيق، سالك للطريق، تارك لهواه، راسخ القدم في خدمة مولاه فإذا وجده فليمتثل ما أمر، ولينته عما نهى عنه وزجر. [«مفتاح الفلاح» ص30]

وقال أيضا: (ليس شيخك من سمعت منه وإنما

شيخك من أخـذت عنه! وليس شيخك من واجهتك عبارته، وإنما شيخك الذي سرت فيك إشارته! وليس شيخك من دعاك إلى الباب، وإنما شيخك الذي رفع بينك وبينه الحجاب! وليس شيخك من واجهك مقاله، إنما شيخك الذي نهض بك حاله! شيخك هو الذى أخرجك من سجن الهوى، ودخل بك على المولى! شيخك هو الذي ما زال يجلو مرآة قلبك، حتى تجلت فيها أنوار ربك! أنهضك إلى الله فنهضت إليه! وسار بك حتى وصلت إليه! وما زال محاذيا لك حتى ألقاك بين يديه! فزج بك في نورالحضرة و قال: ها أنت وربك)[«لطائف المنن» ص167]

وقال أيضا: (لا تصحب من لا ينهضك حاله ولا يدلك على الله مقاله).

وقال الإمام حجة الإسلام أبو حامد الغزالي رحمه الله تعالى:
(كنت في مبدأ أمري منكرا لأحوال الصالحين، ومقامات العارفين، حتى صحبت شيخي (يوسف النساج) فلم يزل يصقلني بالمجاهدة حتى حظيت

بالواردات، فرأيت الله تعالى في المنام، فقال لي: يا أبا حامد دع شواغلك، واصحب أقواما جعلتهم في أرضي محل نظري، وهم الذين باعوا الدارين بحبي. قلت: بعزتك إلا أذقتني برد حسن الظن بهم. قال: قد فعلت، و القاطع بينك و بينهم تشاغلك بحب الدنيا، فاخرج منها مختارا قبل أن تخرج منها صاغرا، فقد أفضت عليك أنوارا من جوار قدسي! فاستيقظت فرحا مسرورا وجئت إلى شيخي، فقصصت عليه المنام، فتبسم و قال: يا أبا حامد هذه ألواحنا في البداية، بل إن صحبتي ستكحل بصيرتك بإثمد التأييد... الخ) [«شخصيات صوفية» لطه عبد الباقي سرور ص154 . توفى سنة 1382] هـ .

و قال أيضا: يحتاج المريد إلى شيخ وأستاذ يقتدى به لا محالة ليهديه إلى سواء السبيل، فإن سبيل الدين غامض، وسبل الشيطان كثيرة ظاهرة فمن لم يكن له شيخ يهديه، قاده الشيطان إلى طرقه لا محالة. فمن سلك سبل البوادي المهلكة بغير خفير فقد خاطر بنفسه وأهلكها، و يكون المستقل بنفسه كالشجرة التي تنبت بنفسها فإنها

تجف على القرب، وإن بقيت مدة وأورقت لم تثمر، فمعتصم المريد شيخه، فليتمسك به («الإحياء» ج3/ ص65).

ولله در القائل:

ما لذة العيش إلا صحبة الفقراء
هم السلاطين و السادات و الأمراء
فاصحبهم و تأدب في مجالسهم
و خل حظك مهما قدموك ورا

وأما السؤال عن طلب الشيخ هل هو فرض على كل فرد أو على البعض دون البعض؟ وما السبب؟ فقد أجاب عنه مولانا القطب المكتوم والخاتم المحمدي المعلوم، سيدي أحمد التجاني، كما نقله عنه سيدي محمد بن المشرى في «روض المحب الفاني»، حيث قال:

الجواب أن طلب الشيخ في الشرع ليس بواجب وجوبا شرعيا يلزم من طلبه الثواب ومن عدم طلبه العقاب. فليس في الشرع شيء من هذه، ولكنه واجب من طريق النظر مثل الظمآن إذا احتاج إلى الماء وإن لم يطلبه هلك، فطلبه عليه

لازم من طريق النظر، وطريق النظر في هذا ما قدمناه من كون الناس خلقوا لعبادة الله والتوجه إلى الحضرة الإلهية بالإعراض عن كل ما سواها.

وعلم المريد ما في نفسه من التثبط والتثبيط عن النهوض إلى الحضرة الالهية، وعلم عجزه عن مقاومة نفسه بما يريده منها من الدخول في الحضرة الالهية بتوفية الحقوق والأدب, وعلم أنه لا ملجأ له من الله ولا منجى إن أقام مع نفسه متبعا لهواها معرضا عن الله تعالى، فإنه بهذا النظر يجب عليه طلب الشيخ الكامل. وهذا الوجوب النظري أمر وضعي طبيعي ليس هو من نصوص الشرع، إذ ليس في نصوص الشرع إلا وجوب توفية القيام بحقوق الله ظاهرا وباطنا على كل فرد من جميع العبيد ولا عذر لأحد في ترك ذلك من طريق الشرع، ولا عذر له في غلبة الهوى عليه، وعجزه عن مقاومة نفسه.

فليس في الشرع إلا وجوب ذلك وتحريم ترك ذلك بوجوب العقاب عليه. فهذا ما كان في الشرع ولا شيخ يجب طلبه إلا شيخ التعليم الذي يعلم

كيفية الأمور الشرعية التي يطلب فعلها من العبيد أمرا ونهيا وفعلا وتركا. فهذا الشيخ يجب طلبه على كل جاهل لا يسع أحدا تركه, وما وراء ذلك من الشيوح لا يلزم طلبه من طريق الشرع لكن يجب طلبه من طريق النظر بمنزلة المريض الذي أعضلته العلة وعجز عن الدواء من كل وجه وانعدمت الصحة في حقه, فنقول إن شاء البقاء على هذا المرض بقي كذلك، وإن طلب الخروج إلى كمال الصحة قلنا له يجب عليك طلب الطبيب الماهر الذي له معرفة بالعلة وأصلها وبالدواء المزيل لها وكيفية تناوله كما وكيفا ووقتا وحالا والسلام.

أدب الكاملين والعارفين المحققين

اتفق المشايخ الكاملون والعارفون المحققون على أن الأدب في طريق أهل الله تعالى اكد كل أمر وجامع لكل خير وبر، و نصوا على أن من لازم سلوك سبيله في جميع ذلك وصل واتصل، ومن حاد عن نهجه انقطع وانفصل، وذلك لأن الطريق آداب كلها، لكل وقت أدب و لكل حال أدب و لكل مقام أدب.

قال صلى الله عليه و سلم « أدبني ربي فأحسن تأديبي ثم أمرني بمكارم الأخلاق».

والأدب هو تهذيب الظاهر و الباطن ، فإذا تأدب ظاهر العبد و باطنه صار أديبا.قال الشيخ محي الدين رضى الله عنه «الأدب جماع الخير».
وقال ابن عطاء:»الأدب الوقوف مع المستحسنات».
قيل له: ما معنى ذلك؟

قال: أن تعامل الله سرا وعلانية بالأدب، فإن كنت كذلك كنت أديبا وإن كنت أعجميا. ثم أنشد :

إذا نطقت جاءت بكل مليحة
وان سكنت جاءت بكل مليح

وما أحسن قول بعضهم في الأدب :
الأدب أن يؤدب العبد ظاهره وباطنه، أما ظاهره فبالشريعة بأن يتبع السنة قولا وفعلا، وأما باطنه فبالحقيقة بأن يرضى بما يرد عليه من الله ويتلقاه بالقبول، ويرى أن الكل نعمة عليه من الله تعالى، إما عاجلة وإما آجلة، فالعاجلة بلوغ النفس محبوها عاجلا، وآلآجلة كأنواع المضار و المكاره، فإنه يثاب عليها آجلا ويحط بها عنه من خطيئاته، فهي نعمة بهذا الاعتبار، وصاحب هذا الأدب هو المخصوص برؤية النعم في طي النقم، فيرى نعم الله تعالى عليه ظاهرة وباطنة.

وجاء في الحديث عن معاذ رضي الله عنه أنه قال: قال رسول الله صلى الله عليه وسلم: «حف الإسلام بمكارم الأخلاق ومحاسن الآداب».

وقال سيدنا أنس بن مالك رضي الله عنه: «الأدب في العمل علامة قبول العمل».

وقال عبد الله بن المبارك رضي الله عنه: «من تهاون بالأدب عوقب بحرمان السنن، ومن تهاون بالسنن عوقب بحرمان الفرائض، ومن تهاون بالقرائض عوقب بحرمان المعرفة».

وقال ذو النون المصرى رضي الله عنه: «إذاخرج المريد عن حد استعمال الأدب فإنه يرجع من حيث جاء».

أما الأدب مع الشيخ فاعتقاد كماله وأنه أهل للشيخوخة والتربية لجمعه بين شريعة وحقيقة وبين جذب وسلوك وأنه على قدم النبي صلى الله عليه وسلم وثانيها تعظيمه وحفظ حرمته غائبا وحاضرا وتربية محبته في قلبه وهو دليل صدقه وبقدر التصديق يكون فمن لا صدق له لا سير له ولو بقي مع الشيخ ألف سنة ويرحم الله سيدي محمدا الشرقي حيث قال (بالمغربية) من لا صدق، ما عند باش ينفق من لا حقق ما جاب إيمارايا بابا.

وأما الآداب مع الأخوان كما ذكره ابن عجيبة: حفظ حرمتهم غائبين أو حاضرين فلا يغتاب أحد ولا ينقص أحدا فلا يقول أصحاب سيدى فلان كمال وأصحاب سيدي فلان نقص أو فلان عارف أو فلان ليس بعارف أو فلان ضعيف وفلا نقوي أو غير ذلك فهذه عين الغيبة وهي حرام بالأجماع لا سيما في حق الأولياء فإن لحومهم سموم قاتلة كلحوم العلماء والصالحين فليحذر المريد جهده من هذه الخصلة الذميمة وليفر ممن هذا طبعه فراره من الأسد فمن أولع بهذا فلا يفلح أبدا فالأولياء كالأنبياء فمن فرق بينهم حرم خيرهم وكفر نعمتهم. وقد قال بعض الصوفية من كسره الفقراء لا يجبره الشيخ ومن كسره الشيخ فقد يجبره الفقراء.

ومن بين ألاداب أيضا إسداء النصح إليهم. وحسن معاشرتهم، والتعامل معهم على مبدأ: «وتعاونوا على البر والتقوى».

يقول مولانا شيخ الاسلام الحاج ابراهيم:

الادب الادب يا ذا السالك

فإنه الباب لكل سالك

وقال أيضا في نفس النظم:

تأدب في ظاهر و باطن

به يرقى المرئ للمواطن

الحيرة والتسليم

وهو الإيمان الكامل الذى لا يعتمد صاحبه التقليد ولا يستكفي بالاستدلال فقط وإنما يعتمد نور البصيرة فى شهود الحضرة الربانية الأزلية الأبدية ويراقبها في كل تصرفاته وحركاته وسكناته.

وقديما قال أحد الأكابر: لا يعرف الله إلا من تعرف إليه ولا يوحده إلا من توحد له ولا يومن به إلا من لطف به ولا يصفه إلا من تجلى لسره ولا يخلص له إلا من جذبه إليه ولا يصلح له إلا من اصطنعه لنفسه.

وقيل: لو أراد الخلق تنزيه الخالق إلا بلسان العجز ما استطاعوا قال صلى الله عليه وسلم:
«لا احصي ثناء عليك أنت كما أثنيت على نفسك»[رواه مسلم واصحاب السنن].

وقد روى الترمذي في نوادر الأصول:
(ان الله تعالى احتجب عن العقول كما احتجب عن الابصار وإن الملأ الأعلى يطلبونه كما تطلبونه).

ولذا يقول الجنيد: انتهى عقل العقلاء إلى الحيرة، وقال ذوالنون: غاية العارفين التحير.

هذا و قد قال الله تعالى: ﴿ويحذركم الله نفسه والله رؤوف بالعباد﴾.

وقال: ﴿وما قدروا الله حق قدره﴾

وقال: ﴿يعلم ما بين أيديهم وما خلفهم ولا يحيطون به علما﴾ و﴿لا يحيطون بشيء من علمه إلا بما شاء﴾

وقال: ﴿ولا تقف ماليس لك به علم إن السمع والبصر والفؤاد كل أولئك كان عنه مسئولا﴾

وقال: ﴿قل إنما حرم ربي الفواحش ما ظهر منها وما بطن والاثم والبغى بغير الحق وأن تشركوا بالله ما لم ينزل به سلطانا وأن تقولوا على الله ما لا تعلمون﴾

وقال: ﴿سبحان ربك رب العزة عما يصفون﴾.

لهذا فالمخلوق أيا كان لا يحد الخالق و لا يدركه باعتبار كنه ذاته وتجرده عن النعوت والتعينات بل الذي يدرك الله ويقدره حق قدره هو الله تعالى وحده لا غيره والعقول الآدمية ضعيفة محدودة لا تدرك من التوحيد و المعرفة إلا افتقار الصنعة إلى صانعها.

وعليه فإن الله لا يؤاخذ الإنسان بما عسر على عقله تصوره او فهمه، و يكفي أن يسلم ويؤمن به. و في هذا المعنى قال البوصيري:

لم يمتحنا بما تعيا العقول به
حرصا علينا فلم نرتب و لم نهم

من هنا يتبين لنا أن المعرفة من فعل القلب لا من فعل العقل.

قال أبو بكر الصديق رضي الله عنه: العجز عن درك الإدراك إدراك.

وفي ذلك يقول العلامة محمد فال ولد يدالي:

الخوض في إدراكه إشراك
والعجز عن ادراكه إدراك
والعجز عن إدراكه الصديق
قال هو الإدراك والتحقيق

الحجاب

روى عن الرسول صلى الله عليه وسلم أنه قال: «إن لله سبعين ألف حجابا من نور وظلمة، لو كشفها لأحرقت سبحات وجهه كل من أدركه بصره».

قلت: لقد أجمع أهل الله على أن هذه الحجب إنما هي باعتبار العبد، لا باعتبار الحق تبارك وتعالى، والدليل على ذلك أن وجه الله تبارك وتعالى لم يحجبه شيء، فهو مطلع على الخلق دائما اطلاعا مباشرا منذ بدء الخليقة، ولم يحترق منها شيء. فلو كانت الحجب له هو، لاحترق العالم بنظرة واحدة منه كما في الحديث. فافهم ذلك.

قال الشيخ الأكبرالامام محيي الدين ابن عربي في كتابه الحجب:

اعلم أيها المحب كائنا من كان أن الحجب التي

بينك و بين محبوبك كائنا من كان ليس شيئا سوى وقوفك مع الأشياء لا للأشياء، كما يقول من لم يذق طعم الحقائق، وانما وقف مع الأشياء لضعف الادراك، وهو عدم النفوذ، وهو المعبر عنه بالحجاب، وهو عدم.

والعدم لا شيء ولا حجاب. ولو كانت الحجب صحيحة لكان من احتجب عنك احتجبت عنه. والعارف ما نذكره إلا من كان الحق سمعه وبصره، وهو الذي يعرف ما يعبر عنه بالحجاب.

واعلم أنك إذا تفرغت لأمر ما بالكلية فالضرورة ان تقف معه، وذلك الوقوف هو حجابك فتتخيل أن الوقوف معه حجبك، وليس كذلك والوقوف مع الخلق حجابك عن الحق، والوقوف مع الحق حجابك مع الخلق. وهذا من باب التوسع والإيناس، كما ورد في الكتاب والسنة من ذكر الحجب النورانية والظلمانية وعلى هذا التوسع ثبتت الحجب.

قال في إيقاظ الهمم:

الحق ليس بمحجوب عنك إنما المحجوب أنت عن النظر إليه إذ لو حجبه شيء لستره ما حجبه، ولو كان له ساتر لكان لوجوده حاصر وكل حاصر لشيء، فهو له قاهر وهو القاهر فوق عباده. قلت: الحق تعالى محال في حقه الحجاب فلا يحجبه شيء لأنه ظهر بكل شيء وقبل كل شيء وبعد كل شيء فلا ظاهر معه ولا موجود في الحقيقة سواه، فهو ليس بمحجوب عنك وإنما المحجوب أنت عن النظر إليه لإعتقادك الغيرية وتعلق قلبك بالأمور الحسية فلو تعلق قلبك بطلب المولى، وأعرضت بالكلية عن رؤية السوى، لنظرت إلى نور الحق ساطعا في مظاهر الأكوان، وصار ما كان محجوبا عنك بالوهم في معد الشهود والعيان.

وفي هذا المعنى قال ابن عطاء الله:
«ما حجبك عن الحق وجود موجود معه إذ لا شيء معه. وإنما حجبك عنه توهم موجود معه!».

قال أحد شعرائهم:
وما احتجبت إلا برفع حجابها
ومن عجب أن الظهور تستر

وقال آخر:

لقد ظهرت فلا تخفي على أحد
إلا على أكمه لا يبصر القمرا
لكن بطنت بما أظهرت محتجبا
وكيف يعرف من بالعزة استترا

وقال في ايقاظ الهمم أيضا: ثم إحتجابه تعالى في حال ظهوره، مما يدلك على وجود قهره، كما أشار إليه في الحكم بقوله:

"مما يدلك على وجود قهره سبحانه إن حجبك عنه بما ليس بموجود معه".

فاحتجب عنهم بشيء ليس بموجود، وهو الوهم، والوهم أمر عدمي مفقود، فما حجبه إلا شدة ظهوره وما منع الأبصار من رؤيته إلا قهارية نوره، فتحصل إنفراد الحق بالوجود وليس مع الله موجود. قال تعالى:

﴿كل شيء هالك إلا وجهه﴾، وأسم الفاعل حقيقة في الحال.

وقال تعالى: ﴿هو الأول والآخر والظاهر والباطن﴾

وقال تعالى: ﴿فأينما تولوا فثم وجه الله﴾

وقال تعالى: ﴿وهو معكم أينما كنتم﴾

وقال تعالى: ﴿وإذ قلنا لك ان ربك أحاط بالناس﴾

وقال تعالى: ﴿وما رميت إذ رميت ولكن الله رمى﴾

وقال تعالى: ﴿إن الذين يبايعونك إنما يبايعون الله﴾

وقال صلى الله عليه وسلم:
أفضل كلمة قالها شاعر كلمة لبيد:
"ألا كل شيء ما خلا الله باطل وكل نعيم لا محالة زائل".

و قال صلى الله عليه و سلم: «سيقول الله تعالى يا عبدي مرضت فلم تعدني، فيقول: يا رب كيف أعودك و أنت رب العالمين؟ فيقول الله: أما أنه مرض عبدي فلان فلم تعده، فلو عدته لوجدتني عنده! ثم يقول: يا عبدي إستطعمتك فلم تطعمني، ثم يقول: أستسقيتك فلم تسقني... الحديث".

فدل الحديث على أن هذه الهياكل والأشخاص خيالات لا حقيقة لها فهي أشبه شيء بالظلال.

وقال مولانا شيخ الإسلام الشيخ إبراهيم نياس في كتابه "كاشف الالباس" :

و أما معرفة كيفية زوال هذا الحجاب فهو السعي في قطع الحظوظ والشهوات وترك تعظيم نفسها و السعي في جلب مصالحها و قطع دفع مضارها بالزهد فيها بالكلية لكن بلطف ورفق. وأما معرفة أصول الحجاب فهو كثرة الأكل و الشرب وملاقاة الخلق وكثرة الكلام وكثرة المنام ودوام الغفلة عن ذكر الله تعالى. و أما السعي والجد في قطع تلك الأصول فهو الجوع والعطش بالرفق ودوام الانقطاع عن ملاقاة الخلق و دوام الصمت مطلقا إلا فيما قل من ضرورياته، ومداومة السهر بالرفق، ومداومة ذكر الله تعالى بالقلب واللسان دائما بأى ذكر.

ثم إن الأذكار التي بها زوال الحجاب منها كليات و هي التي لا تقطع إلا حجابا واحدا من نوع

واحد. أما الكليات فهي لا إله إلا الله ، او الصلاة على رسول الله صلى الله عليه وسلم، أو سبحان الله والحمد لله ، أو الله أكبر ، أو بسم الله الرحمن الرحيم، أو الله الله الله ، او الله لا إله إلا هو الحى القيوم.

وأما التفصيليات فهى سائر الأسماء الحسنى ، وكل اسم يذهب بجزء من الحجاب ولا يتعدى للجزء الآخر. والله تعالى الموفق. اه كلامه الجدير بأن يكتب بذوب الذهب.

قلت: ومن أراد شيئا زائدا على ماذكر هنا مما يقطع الحجاب فعليه بملازمة رجاله، فقد قال السيد العربى بن السائح رضى الله عنه: إن فى جواهر المعاني طرقا عديدة كلها موصلة على الله تعالى . قلت: وما هو مكتوم أكثر من ذلك، و لكن سائق السعادة يسوق أناسا، والصارف الالهى يصرف آخرين.

الماء منهمر والأرض معشبة

أقام فيها مريد الخير أو رحلا

الدخول إلى الحضرة المقدسة

قال ابن عجيبة: الحضرة مقدسة منزهة مرفعة لا يدخلها إلا المطهرون، فحرام على القلب الجنب أن يدخل مسجدا الحضرة، وجنابة القلب غفلته عن ربه.

قال تعالى: ﴿يا أيها الذين آمنوا لا تقربوا الصلاة وأنتم سكارى حتى تعلموا ما تقولون ولا جنبا إلا عابرى سبيل حتى تغتسلوا﴾

أي؛ لا تقربوا صلاة الحضرة وأنتم سكارى بحب الدنيا وشهود السوى، حتى تتيقظوا وتتدبروا ما تقولون في حضرة الملك، ولا جنبا من جماع الغفلة وشهود السوى، حتى تتطهروا بماء الغيب الذى أشار إليه الحاتمي رضي الله عنه كما في الطبقات الشعرانية في ترجمة أبي المواهب بقوله:

تطهربماء الغيب إن كنت ذا سر
و إلا فتيمم بالصعيد أو الصخر
وقدم إما ما كنت أنت إمامه و
صل صلاة الفجر في أول العصر
فهذي صلاة العارفين بربهم
فإن كنت منهم فانضح البر بالبحر

يعني تطهر من شهود نفسك بماء الغيبة عنها بشهود ربك، أو تطهر من شهود الحس بشهود المعنى، أو تطهر من شهود عالم الشهادة بماء شهود عالم الغيب، أو تطهر من شهود السوى، بماء العلم بالله فإنه يغيب عنك كل ما سواه. وإذا تطهرت من شهود السوى تطهرت من العيوب كلها... إلى آخر كلامه.

وقلت قديما في هذا المعني:

وجدت مراد يبعد نفي لغيره
هو الواحد القريب من كل خلقه
فلا شيء غير الحق في كل موقع
تأمل مريد الوصل تفز بوصله

آيات قرآنية، واحاديث نبوية في يبان المعرفة

قال تعالى:

﴿اللَّهُ نُورُ السَّمَاوَاتِ وَالْأَرْضِ مَثَلُ نُورِهِ
كَمِشْكَاةٍ فِيهَا مِصْبَاحٌ الْمِصْبَاحُ فِي زُجَاجَةٍ
الزُّجَاجَةُ كَأَنَّهَا كَوْكَبٌ دُرِّيٌّ يُوقَدُ مِن
شَجَرَةٍ مُّبَارَكَةٍ زَيْتُونِةٍ لَّا شَرْقِيَّةٍ وَلَا غَرْبِيَّةٍ
يَكَادُ زَيْتُهَا يُضِيءُ وَلَوْ لَمْ تَمْسَسْهُ نَارٌ نُّورٌ
عَلَى نُورٍ يَهْدِي اللَّهُ لِنُورِهِ مَن يَشَاءُ وَيَضْرِبُ
اللَّهُ الْأَمْثَالَ لِلنَّاسِ وَاللَّهُ بِكُلِّ شَيْءٍ عَلِيمٌ
* فِي بُيُوتٍ أَذِنَ اللَّهُ أَن تُرْفَعَ وَيُذْكَرَ فِيهَا
اسْمُهُ يُسَبِّحُ لَهُ فِيهَا بِالْغُدُوِّ وَالآصَالِ * رِجَالٌ
لاَّ تُلْهِيهِمْ تِجَارَةٌ وَلاَ بَيْعٌ عَن ذِكْرِ اللهِ وَإِقَامِ
الصَّلاَةِ وَإِيتَاءِ الزَّكَاةِ يَخَافُونَ يَوْماً تَتَقَلَّبُ
فِيهِ الْقُلُوبُ وَالأَبْصَارُ * لِيَجْزِيَهُمُ اللَّه
أَحْسَنَ مَا عَمِلُواْ وَيَزِيدَهُمْ مِّن فَضْلِهِ وَاللَّه

﴿يَرْزُقُ مَن يَشَآءُ بِغَيْرِ حِسَابٍ﴾

قال بعض أهل العلم:

وقد بين سبحانه هذه الحقيقة بأن له تعالى نورا عاما تستنير به السماوات والارض فتظهر به في الوجود بعدما لم تكن ظاهرة فيه، فمن البين أن ظهور شيء بشيء يستدعى كون المظهر ظاهرا بنفسه و(الظاهر بذاته المظهر لغيره هو النور). فهو تعالى نور يظهر السماوات والارض بإشراقه عليها، كما ان الانوار الحسية تظهر الاجسام الكثيفة للحس بإشراقها عليها غير أن ظهور الاشياء بالنور الإلهي عين وجودها وظهور الاجسام الكثيفة بالانوار الحسية غير أصل وجودها.

ونورا خاصا يستنير به المؤمنون ويهتدون إليه بأعمالهم الصالحة وهو نور المعرفة الذي سيستنير به قلوبهم وأبصارهم يوم تتقلب فيه القلوب والابصار فيهتدون به إلى سعادتهم الخالدة فيشاهدون فيه شهود عيان ما كان في غيب عنهم في الدنيا.

ومثل تعالى هذا النور بمصباح في زجاجة في مشكاة يشتعل من زيت في نهاية الصفاء فتتلالا الزجاجة كأنها كوكب دري فتزيد.نورا على نور، والمصباح موضوع في بيوت العبادة التي يسبح الله فيها رجال من المؤمنين لا تلهيهم عن ذكر ربهم وعبادته تجارة ولا بيع.

فهذه صفة ما أكرم الله به المؤمنين من نور معرفته المتعقب للسعادة الخالدة، وحرمه على الكافرين وتركهم في ظلمات لا يبصرون، فخص من اشتغل بربه وأعرض عن عرض الحياة الدنيا بنور من عنده، واللَّه يَفْعَلُ مَا يَشَاءُ لَهُ الْمُلْكُ وَإِلَيه الْمَصِيرُ. وقال الأخفش في معنى قوله تعالى: ﴿وَمَا قَدَرُوا اللَّه حَقّ قَدْرِهِ﴾ [الأنعام:91] أى ما عرفوه حق معرفته، (وللآية وجهان في التفسير).

وانظر يا أخى لقول رسول الله صلى الله عليه وسلم وهو يقول: من عرف نفسه فقد عرف ربه.

قال محي الدين ابن عربي معلقا على هذا الحديث: أشار- صلى الله عليه وسلم - بذلك أنك لست

أنت، - بل - أنت هو بلا أنت: لا هو داخل فيك ولا هو خارج منك، ولا أنت خارج منه ولا أنت داخل فيه؛ ولا بذلك أنك موجود وصفتك هكذا أبدا: غني به.

إنك ما كنت قط ولا تكون، لا بنفسك ولا فيه ولا معه، ولا أنك فان ولا موجود. أنت هو، وهو أنت، بلا علة من هذه العلل فإن عرفت وجودك بهذه الصفة فقد عرفت الله، وإلا فلا. اه.

عن عائشة رضي الله عنها، أن النبي صلى الله عليه وسلم قال: «إن دعامة البيت أساسه، ودعامة الدين المعرفة بالله تعالى، واليقين والعقل القامع فقلت: بأبي أنت وأمي ما العقل القامع؟ قال الكف عن معاصي الله والحرص على طاعة الله». أخرجه الإمام الديلمي.

قال رسول الله صلى الله عليه وسلم: «ذاق طعم الايمان من رضي بالله ربا، والاسلام دينا، وبمحمد صلي الله عليه وسلم نبيا».

قال شاعرهم:

طلعت شمس من أحب ليلا
فاستنارت فما لديها غروب
إن شمس النهار تغرب باليل
وشمس القلوب ليست تغيب

وقال الاخر[ابو مدين]:
الله قل وذر الوجود وما حوى
ان كنت مرتادا بلوغ الكمال
فالغير دون الله ان حققته
عدم على التفصيل والاجمال

وقال العارف:
رأيت ربي بعين قلبي
فقلت لاشك انت انت

وقال الاخر:
رأيت الاله لم ار غير
وكذا الغير عندنا ممنوع

دعوى انقطاع التربية في القرون السالفة ورد صاحب الفيضة عليها

إن مزاعم انقطاع التربية في أيامنا هذه ليست جديدة، فقد قال بها بعض الناس قديما ولا يزال بعض الأذناب يرددها رغم الحجج الدامغة التي دحض بها علماؤنا مزاعمهم، والبراهين القاطعة التي ردوا بها على أوهامهم وأغاليطهم. بل وقد ذهب البعض إلى القول بانقطاء الولاية، وغير ذلك. وقد تكلم مولانا شيخ الاسلام صاحب الفيضة التجانية الشيخ إبراهيم بن الحاج عبد الله نياس عن ذلك في كتاب كاشف الإلباس بإسهاب، وسننقل لكم هنا كلامه ملخصا. قال رضي الله عنه:

قال سيدى زروق في تأسيس القواعد ما نصه: قال شيخنا أبو العباس الحضرمي رضى الله عنه:

ارتفعت التربية بالاصطلاح، ولم يبق إلا الافادة بالهمة والحال، فعليكم باتباع الكتاب والسنة من غير زيادة ولا نقصان الخ ما سيأتي قريبا. وهذا الكلام يفهمه من لا ذوق له ولا علم ولا صدق بأن التربية انقطعت انقطاعا كليا، وذلك فى المائة التاسعة، ولم يرد ذلك ولا شيخهم وإنما مراده كما قال ابن عجيبة العلامة ، شارح الحكم فى إيقاظ الهمم، ونصه: فإن قلت قد قال الحضرمي: قد انقطعت التربية بالاصطلاح وما بقى إلا الهمة والحال فعليكم بالكتاب والسنة، قلت: لم يقصد الحضرمى انقطاعها على الأبد. وحاشا الحضرمي من أن يتحكم على الله ويعجز قدرته. ما أراد أن في زمانه مدعين كثيرين، فحذر أهل زمانه منهم. ومعرفة الحضرمي وزروق رضى الله عنهما تنافى هذا القصد، وعلى تقدير صدورها منهما فليسا لمعصومين، فكل كلام يرد ويقبل إلا كلام صاحب الرسالة صلى الله عليه وسلم، وقد وجد بعد الحضرمى رجال كانوا من أهل التريبة النبوية بالحال والمقال والهمة لا يمكن حصرعددهم، وهم موجودون فى زماننا هذا، مشهورون كنار على علم، قد هدى الله على أيديهم خلقا كثيرا، وخرج على

أيديهم من الأولياء مالا يعلمهم إلا من من الله عليه بمعرفتهم اه منه بلفظ مؤلفه.

ومما يؤيد صاحب الإيقاظ أن القولة صدرت منهما فى القرن التاسع وقبل بروز الختم التجاني حامل راية التربية، ولا يشك في كونه مربيا من له أدنى تصديق أوتسليم، وكذلك الشيخ السيد المختار الكنتى ومن تخرج على يديهما من الرجال الكمل الذين بلغوا مبلغ الشيوخ المربين المرقين.

وذكر شيخنا ووسيلتنا إلى ربنا الختم التجاني رضى الله عنه ما يدل على أن في طريقته وتلامذته مشايخ التربية فى قوله الثابت عنه، و نصه كما فى الجامع:

إذا فتح الله على أصحابي فالذي يجلس منهم عندى في البلد الذى أنا فيه يخاف على نفسه من الهلاك. فقال له بعض أصحابه: منك أو من الله؟ فأجابه: من الله من غير اختيار مني. ذكر هذا فى يوم الأحد الثاني من شهر الله شعبان عام 1224 ثم قال في يوم الاثنين: الخوف المذكور هو على من أذن له من أصحابي في التصرف والتربية للخلق ا ه المراد بلفظه.

ونص كلام سيدى زروق كما فى تأسيس القواعد:

خاتمة: قال شيخنا أبو العباس الحضرمي رضي الله عنه: ارتفعت التربية بالاصطلاح ولم يبق إلا الإفادة بالهمة والحال، فعليكم باتباع الكتاب والسنة من غير زيادة ولا نقصان وذلك جار فى معاملة الحق والنفس والخلق، فأما معاملة الحق فبثلاث: إقامة الفرائض، و اجتناب المحرمات، والاستسلام للحكم. وأما معاملة النفس فبثلاث: الانصاف بالحق، وترك الانتصار لها، والحذر من غوائلها فى الجلب والدفع والرد والقبول والاقبال والأدبار. وأما معاملة الخلق فبثلاث: توصيل حقوقهم لهم، والتعفف عما فى أيديهم، والفرار مما يغير قلوبهم إلا في حق واجب لا محيد عنه.

وكل مريد مال لركوب الخيل أو آثار المصالح العامة ، أو اشتغل بتغيير المنكر في العموم أو التوجه للجهاد دون غيره من الفضائل أو معه حال كونه فى فسحة منه ، أو أراد استيفاء الفضائل أو تتبع عورات إخوانه وغيرهم أو متعللا بالتحذير

أو عمل بالسماع على وجه الدوام أو أكثر الجمع والاطماع لا لتعلم أو تعليم أو مال لأرباب الدنيا بعلة الديانة أو أخذ بالرقائق والدقائق دون المعاملة، وما ينبه عن العيوب، أو تصدى للتربية من غير تقديم شيخ أو امام أو عالم، أو اتباع كل ناعق وقائل بحق أوباطل من غير تفصيل لأحواله، أوإستهان منتسبا لله وإن ظن عدم صدقه بعلامة أو مال للرخص أو التأويلات، أو قدم الباطن على الظاهر أو اكتفى بالظاهر عن الباطن، أو أتى من أحدهما بما لايوافق عليه الآخر أو اكتفى بالعلم عن العمل، أو بالعمل عن الحال والعلم، أو بالحال لاعنهما، ولم يكن له أصل يرجع إليه فى علمه وعمله وحاله وديانته من الأصول المسلمة فى كتب الأئمة ككتب ابن عطاء الله في الباطن، وخصوصا التنوير ومدخل ابن الحاج فى الظاهر وكتاب شيخه ابن أبي جمرة ومن تبعهما من المحققين، فهو هالك لانجاة له، ومن أخذهما فهو ناج مسلم إن شاء الله، والعصمة منه والتوفيق.

وقد سئل رسول الله صلى الله عليه وسلم عن قوله تعالى: عليكم أنفسكم- الآية، فقال : "إذا رأيت

شحا مطاعا، وهوى متبع، وإعجاب كل ذي رأي برأيه فعليك بخويصة نفسك".

وقال عليه الصلاة والسلام: "في صحف إبراهيم: على العاقل أن يكون عارفا لزمنه، ممسكا للسانه، مقبلاعلى شأنه، وعلى العاقل أن يكون له أربع ساعات: ساعة يحاسب فيها نفسه، وساعة يناجى فيها ربه، وساعة يقضى فيها إلى اخوانه الذين يبصرونه بعيوبه ويدلونه على ربه، وساعة خلى فيها بين نفسه وبين شهواتها المباحة". أو كما قال رزقنا الله ذلك وأعاننا عليه ، ووفقنا ، وصحبنا بالعافية فيه ، فإنه لاغنى لنا عن عاقبته، وهو حسبنا ونعم الوكيل وصلى الله على سيدنا ونبينا ومولانا محمد وعلى آله وصحبه وسلم تسليما.

من تأمل كلامه بنفسه من أوله إلى آخره عرف وجه المراد، ولذا قال العارف بالله السيد العربي بن السائح: والمراد بالتربية فى هذا المحط هو التربية بالاصطلاح الذى أحدثه من بعد أهل القرون الثلاثة، وهى التي ذكر الشيخ زروق عن بعض أشياخه أنها انقطعت، وتابعه على ذلك المحقق

اليوسى رحمه الله تعالى، وليس المراد عندهم أن التربية بمعنى الإرشاد بالكتاب والسنة وتلقين الذكر ونحوه، ما يزيح الباطل من النفس ويقطع العلائق والعوائق عنها بسبب استعانتها على ذلك بممدد الشيخ وهمته على حسب ما أذن له من حضرة الله في سره، أو حضرة رسوله صلى الله عليه وسلم يقظة أو مناما قد انقطعت، حاشا أهل الله من ذلك، وانظر الذهب الابريز، انتهى كلامه بلفظه.

قلت : والآيات القرآنية والأحاديث النبوية فيها إشارات وتصريحات فى التبشير بهذه الطائفة الظاهرين على الحق ولم تخص بزمان دون زمان، ولامكان دون مكان، وقال تعالى ﴿وممن خلقنا أمة يهدون بالحق وبه يعدلون﴾ (سورة الأعراف: 181)

قال الشيخ العلامة العارف بالله سيدى الصاوي فى حاشيته على قول الجلال:

وهم أمة محمد صلى الله عليه وسلم كما في الحديث : أى وهوقوله صلى الله عليه وسلم "لاتزال طائفة

من أمتي ظاهرين على الحق إلى أن يأتى أمر الله". وعن معاوية قال وهو يخطب : سمعت رسول الله صلى الله عليه وسلم يقول : " لا تزال من أمتي أمة قائمة بأمر الله لا يضرهم من خذلهم ولا من خالفهم حتى يأتى أمر الله وهم على ذلك".

وهـذه الطائفة لا تختص بزمان دون زمان، ولا مكان دون مكان، بل هم في كل مكان وفى كل زمان، فالإسلام دائما يعلو ولا يعلى عليه، وإن كثر الفساق وأهل الشر فلا عبرة بهم ولا صولة لهم، وفي هذا بشارة لهذه الأمة المحمدية بأن الإسلام في علو وشرف وأهله كذلك إلى قرب يوم القيامة حتى تموت حملة القرآن والعلماء ويقع القرآن من المصاحف وتأتى الريح اللينة فيموت كل من كان فيه مثقال ذرة من الايمان، ولا يكون هذا الأمر إلا بعد وفاة عيسى عليه الصلاة والسلام.

قلت: وفاة عيسى لا تكون الا بعد أن يقتل الدجال ويعيش أربعين عاما. كما تكرر في ذلك الأحاديث، ولا يأتى الدجال إلا بعد المهدى بسبع سنين على رأس مائة. وفى رواية "لا تزال طائفة

بالمغرب"، يعني مقام الختمية والكتمية لأنه محل الأسرار والكتم، وانظر الفتوحات وانظر كتابه الذى سماه "عنقاء مغرب في ختم الأولياء وشمس المغرب". وانظر البغية.

وقال تعالى ﴿ثلة من الأولين وثلة من الآخرين﴾ (سورة الواقعة:40-39).

وروى ابن عباس قال : قال رسول الله صلى الله عليه وسلم " الثلتان من أمتي". انظر الجواهر الحسان. وفي نسيم الرياض لشهاب الدين الخفاجى عند شرحه لحديث "خيركم قرنى ثم الذين يلونهم ثم الذين يلونهم" بعد كلام: فلا ينافيه حديث "أمتي كالمطر لا يدرى الخير في اوله أم في آخره" فإن هذا من واد، وذلك من واد آخر، وهذا إشارة إلى أنه قد يجيء في الأمة من ينفع الناس نفعا عظيما لم يتيسر لغيره ممن سبقه، وهذا بالنظر لأفراد مخصوصة، وذلك بالنظر لمجموع العصر وشتان ما بينهما، ولذا عبر بالقرن. انظر نسيم الرياض.

وقد قال شيخنا ووسيلتنا وقوت أرواحنا وممدنا، القطب الغوث الخاتم المحمدي في قوله تعالى

﴿و ثلة من الآخرين﴾ (سورة الواقعة : 04): هم أصحابنا!

انظر بعين الانصاف تجد له تمام الوراثة حتى صارت في الأمة الثلتان، ثلة لجده وهم أصحاب رسول الله صلى الله عليه وسلم، وثلة له وهم أصحابه رضى الله عنه، وبقي من الاشارات ما أحجم قلمي عن كتبه.

وفي السر أسرار دقاق لطيفة
تراق دمانا جهرة لو بها بحنا

وبهذا تعلم أن انقطاع مدد النبي صلى الله عليه وسلم أو انتقاص نور نبوته لا يقوله من
له أدنى مرتبة من مراتب الإيمان.

وقال شيخنا رضى الله عنه كما في الجامع والجواهر:

اعلم أنه كان صلى الله عليه وسلم يلقى الأحكام العامة للعامة في حياته: يعني إذا حرم شيئا حرمه على الجميع. وإذا افترض شيئا افترضه على الجميع، و كذلك سائر الأحكام الشرعية الظاهرة. ومع

ذلك كله كان صلى الله عليه وسلم يلقى الخاصة للخاصة،وكان يخص ببعض الأمور بعض الصحابة دون بعض وهو شائع ذائع في أخباره صلى الله عليه وسلم. فلما انتقل إلى الدار الآخرة وهو كحياته فى الدنيا سواء، صار يلقى إلى أمته الأمر الخاص للخاص ولا مدخل للأمر العام للعام، فإنه انقطع بموته صلى الله عليه وسلم وبقى فيضه للأمر الخاص للخاص. ومن توهم أنه صلى الله عليه وسلم انقطع جميع مدده على أمته كسائر الأموات فقد جهل رتبة النبي صلى الله عليه وسلم، وأساء الأدب معه، ويخشى عليه أن يموت كافرا إن لم يتب من هذا الاعتقاد. اهـ منه بلفظه.

الطريقة التجانية والسير نحو المعرفة

إن طريقة سيدي أحمد التجاني رضي الله عنه كغيرها من طرق أهل الله، هدفها هو إيصال المريد إلى الله تبارك وتعالى، والأخذ بيده أثناء سلوكه حتى يدخل الحضرة الالهية. هذا هو دأب كل الطرق إلا أن الطريقة الأحمدية المحمدية التجانية تميزت عن سائرها بكثرة بركاتها، وقوة شعاعها، ودوام أنوارها، وكيف لا وهي طريقة ختم الأولياء، ناهيك عن البشائر والذخائر التي انطوت عليها، والتي بشر بها رسول الله صلى الله عليه وسلم سيدنا أبي العباس رضي الله عنه.

هذا وبعد تفجر ينابيع المعارف التجانية، وفيضان عيونها، على يد صاحبها رضي اللهعنه، هرع الناس إليه وأقبلوا عليه ودخلوا أفواجا أفواجا في الطريقة على يديه، حتى أقر العدو قبل الصديق بأن هذا هو

صاحب الفيضة المشار إليه. ولما كان هو صاحبها بحق، فقد ربى ورقى، وأفنى وأبقى، وصفى ونقى حتى أدخل الجمع الغفير إلى حضرة معبودهم، وأوقفهم على مولاهم، وكان ذلك همه وشغله الشاغل. قال رضي الله عنه:

والأمة قصدي فيهم أن أسوقهم
إلى حضرة المولى الكريم إلهنا

وقد مدحه اخوه العلامة الفهامة محمد زينب نياس بقصيدة قال فيها :

الفى طريقة شيخنا التجاني
بقطرنا ساقطة المباني
الفى طريق شيخنا المكنون
قد بيع بالاموال والعيون
فرم من بنيانه ما قد هدم
وطال في الجو بناء كالعلم

هذا وقد نظف الطريقة التجانية من جمع الشوائب والبدع، ودافع عنها أمام المغرضين الضالين المضلين، كما رسم لنا طريقا بينا في التربية

الروحية، من سارعليه وصل دون عناء. وقال رضي الله عنه عن هذه الطريقة:

"ان تركيب ورد هذه الطريقة وحده يربي، لأنه مركب من الاستغفار، والصلاة على النبي, والهيللة. فالاستغفار معناه التخلي عن الذنوب والرذائل، والصلاة على النبي التحلي بالفضائل، ولا إله إلا الله التجلي، حيث يتجلى الله تبارك وتعالى على لسان عبده بقوله؛ لا إله إلا الله، أو إلا أنت، أو إلا أنا".

فانظر هذا الكلام تعرف أنه لا يمكن أن يصدر إلا عن عارف متحقق، وعلامة مدقق، رضي الله عنه وأرضاه.

وأما عن تفاصيل ما تدور عليه التربية في طريقنا فقد أورد ذلك بشكل وافي في كتابه "كاشف الإلباس" حيث قال:

ومدار التربية التجانية دائرة على قطبين: الأول إقامة الصلوات الخمس بشروطها. والثانى الصلاة على النبي آناء الليل وأطراف النهار بنية امتثال

الأمر والتعظيم الإجلال والمحبة، وهذا بعد التزام الورد اللازم الذى يصح به قوام تجانيتك. قال الشيخ الأجل والقدوة المبجل أبو المواهب السيد العربى بن السائح كما في البغية ما نصه: ومدار التربية والتزكية في طريقتنا هذه المحمدية الشريفة المرضية على إمامة الورد الأصلي المعلوم الذى لا يصح الدخول فيها بدونه لأحد من الخصوص ولا من العموم وكذا توابعه من الأذكار المشمولة باللزوم معه وهى الوظيفة المعروفة وذكرالهيللة بعد عصر يوم الجمعة بالمحافظة في جميع ذلك على الشروط المشروطة والآداب التي هي بغاية الحسن ونهاية الكمال منوطة وآكد الشروط وأعظمها المحافظة على الصلوات الخمس بآدابها على الحد المحدود لها شرعا بقدر الامكان واستكمال شروطها وآدابها، وتمام جميع ما لها من الأركان، ثم عمارة مايقدر على عمارته من الأوقات والساعات بالصلاة على النبي صلى الله عليه وسلم خصوصا بصلاة الفاتح لما اغلق التي هى من أسمى الذخائر وأسنى البضاعات على طريق المحبة والشكر والاعتماد على الفضل المحض الذى ليس إلا عليه فى بساط التحقيق المعول من غير التزام خلوة ولا كثرة مجاهدة ولا

غير ذلك مما اصطلح عليه في التربية من بعد الصدر الأول إذ هذه هى طريقة سيدنا رضي الله عنه التي سلكها وامره بالتسليك بها سيد الوجود ومنبع الإمداد والجود صلى الله عليه وسلم.

وفي جواهرالمعاني: بعد ما اعلم سيدنا رضى الله عنه بأنه هو الواسطة بينه وبين الله تعالى والممد له على التحقيق، وصرح له بأنه هو كفيله ومربيه دون غيره من مشايخ الطريق، واخبره أنه لا منة لواحد منهم عليه، لأن جميع ما يصله من الله تعالى فعلى يده صلى الله عليه وسلم بواسطته ومنه إليه.

قال في وصيته التي أوصاه بها: الزم هذه الطريقة من غير خلوة ولا اعتزال عن الناس حتى تصل مقامك الذى وعدت به وأنت على حالك من غير ضيق ولا حرج ولا كثرة مجاهدة. ويرحم الله تعالى العارف البوصيري رضى الله عنه حيث قال في داليته :

والفصل ليس يناله متوسل
بتورع حرج ولا يتزهد

إن قيل ذاك هو الدواء فقل له كحل
الصحيح خلاف كحل الأرمد
يمشي المصرف حيث شاء وغيره
يمشي بحكم الحجر مشي مصفد

وقال في الجواب الشافي: فلم يبق لمن ساقه سائق السعادة إلى الدخول في هذه الطريق الأحمدية وجذبه جاذب العناية إلى الانخراط فى سلك أهل هذه السلسلة المحمدية، وأهلها لله تعالى بفضله بمشاهدة هذه الخصوصية العظمى، وأوقعه بجوده على هذا الكنز الأعظم والذخر الأسمى، إلا أن يلقى القياد إلى هذا الأستاذ الأعظم. ويختم على بابه ويعتكف على أعتابه على طريق المحبة والتسليم وسلب الإرادة له والتحكيم، ويداوم على ورده المحمدى الشريف بالمحافظة التامة على شروطها المشروطة، والوقوف بغاية الجهد عند حدوده المضبوطة حتى يأذن الله تعالى له بالفتح وهو على حاله من غير خلوة ولا مجاهدة ولا غير ذلك من وجوه الرياضات المعروفة فى اصطلاح من بعد الصدر الأول.

فإنه إن داوم عليه على الوجه الموصوف إما أن يفجأه الفتح أو يهجم عليه هجوما، وإما أن يمن الله تعالى عليه برفع الحجاب عن عينى قلبه فيصير يجتمع بروحانية الشيخ رضى الله عنه أو روحانية النبي صلى الله عليه وسلم، فتكون تربيته بطريق الاستفاضة من أحدهما أو منهما معا {ذلك فضل الله يؤتيه من يشاء والله ذو الفضل العظيم } (سورة المائدة : 45) وما في جواهر المعاني من اشتراط استحضار صورة الشيخ رضى الله عنه أو صورة النبي صلى الله عليه وسلم حال ذكر الورد يشير إلى هذا المعنى لمن قدر على ذلك، وقد بسط الكلام فى ميزاب الرحمة الربانية في بيانها. وإما أن يقيض الله له أخا في الطريق يقوم يأعباء تربيته، يشهده الله تعالى سر خصوصيته، ويزيل بينه وبينه حجاب بشريته، فيسير به إلى الله تعالى فى سره وعلانيته ا ه منه بلفظه.

ومن كان فتحه على الوجوه المذكورة يكون نوره تاما، لأن الفتح بحسب المتبوع كما قال الشيخ زروق: فتح كل أحد ونوره على حسب فتح متبوعه ونوره. فمن أخذ عن نصوص الكتاب والسنة،

ففتحه ونوره تام إن تأهل لأخذه منهما، ولكن فاته نور الاقتداء وفتحه، ولذلك تحفظ الأئمة عليه حتى قال ابن المدينى رحمه الله : كان ابن مهدى يذهب لقول مالك، ومالك يذهب لقول سليمان بن يسار، وسليمان يذهب لقول عمر بن الخطاب، فمذهب مالك إذا مذهب عمر رضى الله عنه.

وقال الجنيد رحمه الله : من لم يسمع الحديث ويجالس الفقهاء ويأخذ أدبه عن المتأدبين أفسده من اتبعه، قال الله تعالى : ﴿قل هذه سبيلي أدعوا إلى الله على بصيرة أنا ومن اتبعني﴾ (سورة يوسف :108) الآية.

و قال عز من قائل ﴿ولا تتبعوا السبل فتفرق بكم عن سبيله﴾ (سورة الأنعام :153)

ولا بأس أن نورد هنا بعض اشعارنا فى هذا المحط لما اشتملت عليه من الإشارات التي تربى الصادق، بعضها في حق السالك، وبعضها في حق المجذوب،

فمن ذلك قولنا :

فدع عنك المغاني والغواني
ودع عنك الموائد والمباني
وصاحب كل قرم حاز
جمع الشر يعة والحقيقة غير وان
أخا ورع وزهد ليس يلفى
له هم يزيد على التفان
وحاذر من هوى نفس و
حاذر أخا ميل له مر الأوان
وملكه القياد وأنت تدرى
بأن ما فوقه فى الشأن ثان
تحقق أنه قد دك جهرا
وأوصله المقدس بالتدانى
وقربه وقدسه ونادى له
بالأذن مقول كل دان
ليهنئك الوصول متى تراه
و رؤيته أعز لدى العيان
صلاة الله يصحبها سلام
على المختار من تال وثان

ولنا أيضا :

وإنما الفتح لدى الايمان
تركك ما سواه بالايقان

ولنا أيضا :

فلاينبغي للواصلين تصدر
قبيل وجود الأذن فالسر يستر
ويعجبني الصمت الطويل فإنه
دليل على العرفان والحال مخبر
ولاخيرفي التعبير في كل محفل
قد انتقل الأسرار من حيث يجهر
رعانا إله العرش بالسر سره
عليه صلاة الله فهو المدبر

ومن أراد شيئا زائدا على هذا فعليه بمصاحبة الرجال ، وخدمة أهل الكمال!

هكذا أورد رضي الله عنه وعنا به آمين.

نفحات الأنوار من أقوال بعض أهل الله الكبار

إن تجلي نور شمس الذات الإلهية في مرآة قلب السالك إلى الله، اللاهث وراء الحق، هذا النور قد طرد أنوار الازهرة والقمر والشمس، ورمي بهن في هوة العدم الحالكة. حيث يمحي كل وجود ونور؛ كما في قوله تعالى:» إِذَا الشَّمْسُ كُوِّرَتْ * وَإِذَا النُّجُومُ انكَدَرَتْ«. ولان هذه القيامة عند السالك إلى الله هي واقعة لا محالة، وهي صورة للقيامة الكبرى، فإنه إذا ظهرت علامات ساطعة، تلاشت أنوارالوجود الخيالي المجازي للكائنات، وذابت في وهج إشعاع نور ذات الله المطلقة، و بالظهور المطلق للحق تعالى، تقوم القيامة، ويفنى كل وجود غير وجوده المقدس، وما كان آجلا عند غيره، أصبح عاجلا عنده.

قال في الإيقاظ : علامة كمال العارف وآدابه في

الطلب وفي البسط والقبض وفي المنع والعطاء ومن جملة العطاء ما يعطيه الحق سبحانه عباده من الخيرات في مقابلة أعمالهم الصالحات.

ولما كانت شمس النهار إذا ظهرت لم تشاهد النجوم فكذلك شمس المعرفة إذا أشرقت أفنت الآثار والرسوم و لم يبق إلا الحي القيوم.

قيل :

فلما استبان الصبح أدرج ضوؤه
بإسفاره أضواء نور الكواكب

وقيل أيضا :

لم يبق بيني وبين الحق تبياني
ولا دليل ولا آيات برهان
هذا تجلي شموس الحق نائرة
قد أزهرت في تلاليها بسلطان
لا يعرف الحق إلا من يعرفه لا
يعرف القدمي المحدث الفاني
لا يستدل على الباري بصنعته
و أنتم حدث ينبي بازمان

هذا عبارة أهل الانفراد به

ذوي العارف في سر وإعلان

كلام الشيخ أحمد التجاني في بعض المشاهدات

قال القطب المكتوم سيدي أحمد التجاني في معنى الحديث «لا يزال عبدي يتقرب إلي بالنوافل حتى أحبه، فإذا أحببته كنت سمعه الذي يسمع به .. إلخ» :

«حتى أحبه» معناه: أن محبة الله للعبد هو إفاضة محبة ذاته المقدسة عليه، فهي غاية الغايات، وإليها ينتهي سير كل سائر من وصلها كملت له مطالب الدنيا والآخرة. قال: حتى أحبه، يعني؛ أفيض عليه محبة ذاتي على حد قوله تعالى: ﴿يحبهم وتحبونه﴾ ، فلولا محبته سبحانه وتعالى لهم ما وصلوا إلى محبة ذاته.

وقوله «فإذا أحببته كنت سمعه...الخ» يشهد العبد من نفسه قوة إلهية كأنه هو الذات المقدسة بجميع

صفاتها وأسمائها، كأنه هو وليس هو، ولكنه سبحانه وتعالى أفاض عليه من أنوار صفاته وأسمائه لعلو مقامه، إنما يحمله ما لا يحمله جميع الخلق من الثقل حتى قال بعض العارفين:

من كشف له عن ذرة من التوحيد حمل السماوات والأرضين على شعرة من أجفان عينيه لأنه نهض في هذا المقام بالقوة الألهية، فهو ينظر بالله، كأن ذاته ذات الله تعالى، ويسمع بالله وعلامة النظر والسمع بالله، ففي النظران ينظر الوجود كله من عرشه إلى فرشه من حيث أن لا يخفى منه ذرة واحدة ويستوي أمرها فيما كان خلفه وأمامه ويمينه وشماله وفوقه وتحته، يرى ذلك في الآن الواحد دفعة واحدة ويراه كالجوهر الفرد الذي لا يقبل القسمة فلاتختلط عليه المرئيات وإن اختلفت أحوالها وأوضاعها، و حركاتها وألوانها، كلها يراها على ما هي عليه دفعة واحدة في الآن الواحد في كل جهة من جهاته فلا تختلط عليه ذرة واحدة. وسبب هذه الرؤية أن بصر الروح قد انفتح، فإذا انفتح بصر الروح في ذاته طالع جميع الأكوان والعوالم فلا تختلط عليه الرؤية، فهذا هو النظر بالله تعالى. والسمع بالله

تعالى أن يسمع جميع ألفاظ الوجود في جميع العوالم واختلاف تسبيحها وأفكارها في الآن الواحد فلا تختلط عليه كثرة ألفاظها وتسبيحها كأنه في كل لفظ لا يسمع غيره. فإن أمر العامة في السماع لا يسمع إلا لفظا واحدا فإذا كثرت عليه الألفاظ عجز عن تمييزها. والسالك في هذه الحالة يسمع جميع ألفاظ الموجودات وتسبيحها فلا تختلط عليه. انتهى. من جواهر المعاني.

كلام شيخ الإسلام مولانا إبراهيم نياس في «التجلي الصوري»

فالتجلي الصوري ثلاثة مراتب؛ السفلي منها أول ما يترآ للمريد المشرف على الوصول يشاهد الوجود المجازي عين الوجود الحقيقي رأي التجلي فى المرآة، ولم يشاهد المرآة ولا التجلي فيها، والوسطى ما يشاهده العارفون بعد صحو وبقاء يشهدون الحق على صورة مستحيلة. قال ابن فارض:

وإياك والإعراض عن كل صورة
من مموهة أو حالة مستحيلة

والعليا ما شاهد رسول الله صلى الله عليه وسلم ليلة الإسراء، رآه على صورة أمرد وأما الذات فهي الوجود المطلق الذي إذا ترقى المريد عن ذلك التجلي الصورى، ووصل إلى البطون الذاتي حيث لا مرآة

ولا متجلي ولا متجلى له، وصل إليه، جاءالحق وزهق الباطل. إن الباطل كان زهوقا. وذات الذات هي حضرة الحجاب الأعظم أم الفيض الروح الأكبر، ولسر الذات والوجود الثاني ووجود الوجود، ومدد الوجود ونور الوجود، والحقيقة المحمدية والأحدية، تجلي الذات لنفسها بنفسها لا نسبة فيه إلا هو الله أحد.

والواحدية تجلي الذات للحقيقة المحمدية، ومعرفة سر الظهور والبطون أن يعرف العبد أن الظهور هو البطون والبطون هو الظهور، وذلك بأن تعلم أن الظهور تظاهر فافهم جدا.

والأزل عبارة عما لم يزل قط، والأبد عبارة عما لا يزال عوض، والأزل هو الأبد والأبد هو الأزل، وهو حضرة بقاء سر الحضرات. وأما عالم الغيب فهي قسيم الشهادة، ولعل تفسيرهما؛ أن يقع في بعض أجوبتك عند كلامي في عالم الخلق والأمر. والكون مظهر الألوهية، أي: المألوه في العالم المجازي محقه الوجود الحقيقي، أي؛ العبد.

الرب حق والعبد حق
يا ليت شعري من المكلف
إن قلت عبد فالعبد ميت
أو قلت رب أني يكلف

لكن الحق أن الرب ليس بعبد، والعبد ليس برب، وذلك الذي يصح أن يكون عبدا هو الكون، والشوق حال محبة ووجد كتهالك يرد على قلب العبد من حضرة القهر الذاتي يسلبه عن جميع اختياراته، تارة في جناب الحق، وتارة في جناب مولانا رسول الله صلى الله عليه وسلم، وتارة في شيخه، والماهية الهيولي، أي؛ الذات الساذج، وبحر العمى والطمس من حيث ما هي هي. والهوية: حضرة هو هو، وهو عند العارفين من أسماء الذات تفهم حضرتها من قوله تعالى: ذلك بأن الله هو الحق. والسكر ما يعتري المجذوب في حال غيبته عن الأكوان، وحضوره مع الحق. والمحبة تعلق القلب بالذات العلية شغفا بها لذاتها لا لغرض ولا تكون إلا لكمل العارفين. جعلنا الله منهم بمنه. وهذا مختصر الجواب.

الخاتمة

ونختم هذا الحديث الشيق - والذى لا يرجى ختامه - يذكر كلام للختم التجاني رضي الله، وهو كلام لا تجده في الكتب، قال رضي الله عنه:

«دفعت من الحضرة الالهية دفعة فصار أولي آخري، وآخرى أولي، وكلي جزئي، وجزئي كلي، فصرت أنا هو وهو أنا من حيث هو لا من حيث أنا، وحينئذ لو سئلت عن ألف ألف مسألة لأجبت عنها بجواب واحد، إذ صرت كالمصباح».

وعلق شيخ الإسلام مولانا الشيخ إبراهيم نياس رضي الله عنه على ذلك قائلا:

«هذا الكلام هو سبب كوني أرضى أن يكون هو شيخي رضي الله عنه...»

ولا شك أن مثل هذا الكلام لا يصدر إلا عن عين الولاية رضي الله عنه، ولا غرو فقائله هو العلم الأشهر والقطب الانور، والنجم الازهر، فريد دهره، ووحيد عصره، العلامة الفهامة، مولانا شيخ الإسلام الحاج ابراهيم بن الحاج عبد الله التجاني رضي الله عنه.

وأود أن أذكر لكم هنا مشهدا من مشاهد هذا القطب الهمام لنختم به هذا المقال، حتى يكون ختامه مسك. قال رضي الله عنه:

«وقعة وقعت للعبد الذليل كاتبه عام 1350 هجرية محمدية عليها الصلاة والسلام، وهي؛ أني مكثت مائة ألف سنة من أيام الرب وأنا أسمع الكلام الأزلي الأصفى مواجهة، فتحيرت واضطربت لما اجتمع عندي من اللذة والألم، فإذا أني اندفعت إلى حضرة أشاهد فيها حقيقة حقيقة حقيقة الحقيقة ذاتا بحثا وطمسا في عمى، ولم يبق شعور بمحسوس، فمكثت في هذا مائتي ألف سنة، فإذا أني بشيء أي؛ وجود متميز عني كالظلال وكالدخان، فطلبت ذلك الوجود، فإذا أنا برسول من الذات عبد الذات

وسرها، وهو يقرب مني ويدنو مني حتى غبت فيه فصار عيني، فصرت أطرب لأبي حبيب الذات وسرها وعبدها ومرادها ومرتبتها الجامعة المتجلى لها بكمال الذات. ومكثت في طربي ألف ألف سنة، فجلت في الغيب لم أجد للذات عبدا سواي، وجلت في غيب الغيب فشاهدت جلالا في جمال فإذا بحضرة غيب الغيب تدعوني وتسميني يا أحمد التجاني، فتيقنت أن لا مراد للحق بعد السر إلا أنا، وصاحبت عبد الذات ونصرته و وازرته ألفي ألف سنة فجعلني أبا البشر، ومدد جميع الكائنات، وسر الموجودات، وآدم الأرواح والأشباح. فحملت الأمانة، ونوديت يا داوود إنا جعلناك خليفة في الأرض، فنظرت إلى الأرض فرأيتها على حالها، وإذا بالعوالم الحسية والمعنوية والملأ الأعلى والأسفل والسماء بنيناها بأيد وإنا لموسعون. والأرض فرشناها فنعم الماهدون. ومن كل شيء خلقنا زوجين اثنين لعلكم تذكرون. ففروا إلى الله إني لكم منه نذير مبين. ولا تجعلوا مع الله إلها آخر إني لكم منه نذير مبين. فرجعت إلى حسي وإذا مدة الواقعة كما بين الشفع والوتر، فسبحان الله العظيم، يخص من شاء بما شاء، لا معقب لحكمه،

ولا يسئل عما يفعل وهم يسألون. أ هـ

وبهذا أود أن أختم هذا الحديث الشيق، وأسأل الله تبارك وتعالى أن يجعلنا من أهل معرفته والفهم عنه، وأن يجعلنا من خواص الخواص، الفانين فيه إذا أفناهم، والباقين به إذا أبقاهم، وأن يحفظنا فيما غبنا عنه، وألا يكلنا إلى أنفسنا فيما حضرناه، كما نسأله جل جلاله أن يحفظ هذه البلاد من ويلات الحروب، ومن كل نزاع وشقاق، وأن يؤلف بين قلوب شعبه، ويوحدهم على وطنية راسخة، تنبذ خلفها كل أسباب التفرق والتشرذم. وأن يعفو عمن قضوا في تلك الدوامة الدامية. إنه قريب مجيب الدعوات.

كما نسأله بحضرتي النبوة والولاية وبخليفتهما أن يهب لنا من المعرفة بقدر وسع ربوبيته و أن يملأ ايدينا بالعافية وقلوبنا بالله تبارك وتعالى و أن يعيد علينا هذا المولد ونحن جميعا على احسن حال دينا ودنيا.

اللّٰهُمَّ صل على سيدنا محمد الفاتح لما أغلق والخاتم

لما سبق ناصر الحق بالحق والهادي إلى صراطك المستقيم وعلى آله حق قدره ومقداره العظيم.

سبحان ربك رب العزة عما يصفون وسلام على المرسلين والحمد لله رب العالمين.

وأخيرا اشكر كل الذين ساهموا في اتمام هذا المولد وعلى رأسهم الشريف عمر بن عبد العزيز وأخوته الشرفاء وكل من ساعدهم أو سعى في انجاح هذه الحفلة.

مولد مبارك وسعيد! وكل عام وانتم بخير! كما نسأله أن يوفق ولاة الامور هنا في ساحل العاج و أن يبارك هذه الأرض الميمونة وأن تبقى مباركة طيبة رخاء سخاء لا دنك فيها والسلام.

جمعها راجي رضا ربه وعفوه وتوفيقه؛
الإمام الشيخ التجاني سيس
إمام المسجد الجامع بمدينة كولخ المحروسة
لعشر خلون من شوال عام 1432هـ

What the Knowers of Allāh Have Said About the Knowledge of Allāh

The Original Arabic